HOSPICE IN AMERICA

HOSPICE IN AMERICA

Josefina Bautista Magno December 28,1919–July 27,2003

Josefina B. Magno MD

with Foreword by Derek Doyle, OBE, MD, FRCSE, FRCPE, FRCGP (Scotland), Founder Member and Adviser IAHPC

iUniverse, Inc.
New York Lincoln Shanghai

HOSPICE IN AMERICA

Copyright © 2007 by Josefina B. Magno Trust

All rights reserved. No part of this book may be used or reproduced by any means, graphic, electronic, or mechanical, including photocopying, recording, taping or by any information storage retrieval system without the written permission of the publisher except in the case of brief quotations embodied in critical articles and reviews.

iUniverse books may be ordered through booksellers or by contacting:

iUniverse
2021 Pine Lake Road, Suite 100
Lincoln, NE 68512
www.iuniverse.com
1-800-Authors (1-800-288-4677)

Because of the dynamic nature of the Internet, any Web addresses or links contained in this book may have changed since publication and may no longer be valid.

The views expressed in this work are solely those of the author and do not necessarily reflect the views of the publisher, and the publisher hereby disclaims any responsibility for them.

ISBN: 978-0-595-45651-2 (pbk)
ISBN: 978-0-595-90041-1 (cloth)
ISBN: 978-0-595-89953-1 (ebk)

Printed in the United States of America

To Saint Joseph, my patron saint

To the memory of my husband, Dr. Cesar P. Magno To my sons and daughter: Jose, Vicente, Cesar Jr., Nanette, Carlo and Manolo

To the memory of my son Mario

To the memory of Rev. Timothy Healy, S.J., president of Georgetown University in 1976, who encouraged me to venture into the then unknown world of hospice care

To my mentors: Dame Cicely Saunders of St. Christopher's Hospice; Dr. Kathleen Foley of Sloan Kettering Memorial Cancer Center; Professor Eric Wilkes of St. Luke's Nursing Home Hospice in Sheffield, England; Dr. Derek Doyle of St. Columba's Hospice in Edinburgh, Scotland; and Dr. Balfour Mount of Royal Victoria Hospital in Montreal

To my many friends and colleagues in the hospice community of America who helped and supported me in this journey of many years

"We are all God's children, so it is important to share His gifts. Do not worry about why problems exist in the world-just respond to people's needs."

—*Mother Teresa*

Contents

Foreword... xiii
Preface xv
Chronology... xvii
CHAPTER 1   What is hospice................................. 1
CHAPTER 2   The journey begins 5
CHAPTER 3   The man I married 11
CHAPTER 4   Crossing the ocean.............................. 21
CHAPTER 5   The house on Military Road 25
CHAPTER 6   Yes, it is cancer 30
CHAPTER 7   The seed of hospice 34
CHAPTER 8   Learning hospice at St. Christopher's........... 38
CHAPTER 9   "Do whatever you need to do"................... 42
CHAPTER 10   The Hospice of Northern Virginia 48
CHAPTER 11   "How long, Doctor?"............................ 57
CHAPTER 12   "I want to be alive until I die" 62
CHAPTER 13   The Woodlawn Center 66
CHAPTER 14   "Out of the hearts of people who care" 70
CHAPTER 15   Involving the physicians 84
CHAPTER 16   Hospice for profit 89

CHAPTER 17	The move to Michigan............................	92
CHAPTER 18	Henry Ford Hospital Hospice	97
CHAPTER 19	My son Mario	100
CHAPTER 20	Hospice in the Philippines	111
CHAPTER 21	My spiritual journey................................	121

ACKNOWLEDGMENTS

I thank Monina Allarey Mercado, my editor and esteemed friend, for her guidance, patience, enthusiasm, sensitivity and very hard work which made this book what it is; my special thanks to my sister Teresita B. Coronel and my daughter-in-law Margaret Day Magno, for their help with the manuscript; my thanks also to Jose Guerra and Lilette Ligon for providing the motivation for this book and for reviewing the first drafts; my thanks to my dear colleagues, William Farr, M.D., and Alexander Peralta, M.D., for their continuing support and faithfulness through the years which helped make this book possible; and in a very, very special way, my gratitude to my dear friend, Helena Metzger, for her friendship and for being my companion in the many ups and downs of my spiritual journey.

FOREWORD

Fame is a curious thing. It comes to few in their lifetime and in most cases is not sought, forever remains a mystery to them, and can even be an embarrassment; such is their natural modesty. Perhaps the word distinction is preferable to fame for such people. It distinguishes them from the attention-seekers, the personally ambitious and the media-manipulators. The truly distinguished in our midst are few in number and deserve the fame they never craved.

Jo Magno is one such. Born in the Philippines she gained her medical degree there and subsequently pursued post-graduate studies in New York and Washington to enable her to practice oncology, and hematology in particular. Like many others before her she became deeply and painfully aware that the dying in our midst were a disadvantaged group, suffering quite unnecessarily in spite of all the advances in modern medicine. Out of this grew her commitment to hospice care. Aware of the work and example of Dame Cicily Saunders in London, a charismatic person with whom Jo Magno is understandably compared, she then went to St. Christopher's Hospice in London to gain the experience she knew she needed, and subsequently worked in Sheffield, Montreal and Oxford, all pioneering centers of excellence and example in the evolving field of hospice and palliative care.

Even today, though certainly less than used to be the case, there are some who see hospice as unscientific, appropriate for nurses and counselors but not for highly trained, frenetically busy doctors. From the beginning of her crusade (for there is no better word to describe it) Jo Magno refuted that by her own example and invited her colleagues, far and near, to join her in what she regarded as the ultimate challenge ever faced by a caring doctor-compassionate and skilled care for the dying.

She brought to her work more than academic distinction and clinical skills. She brought a simple faith, which never seemed to waiver, even when she lost her husband and was left to bring up seven children, one of whom has also died of cancer. Finally, to her skills and her convictions were now added that mystical extra, possessed by so few but seen in abundance in Jo Magno, charisma. Achievement and distinction, though never sought by her, were assured.

She was instrumental in establishing the International Hospice Institute (IHI) from which has grown many other professional bodies promoting hospice and palliative care in the United States. Others might have been content to see hundreds of medical colleagues being attracted to this work, or ministry as she would call it, but her eyes then rested on the needs of those in less fortunate countries than her adopted one. Under her influence the IHI became the International Hospice Institute and College (IHIC), dedicated to promoting hospice and palliative care worldwide.

Her name and her example are known and respected throughout the world of hospice care. Lesser mortals would, by now, have retired to enjoy their grandchildren. Others would have enjoyed watching their protégés following in their footsteps. Not Jo Magno. We are indebted to her doctor, someone with more courage and persuasive power than most of us possess, who ordered her to rest and suggested she write a book. Her recovery of health is, like her life's work, our gain.

—*Derek Doyle, M.D.*

PREFACE

The modern hospice concept of care originated in England through the pioneering efforts of Dame Cicely Saunders. It found its way to the United States because people felt the need to provide appropriate care for those patients for whom cure of disease is no longer possible. In the words of US Senator Edward Kennedy of Massachusetts, who gave the keynote address at the first National Hospice Organization meeting held in Washington, D.C., in November 1978 "hospice care was not mandated by the federal government, nor was it legislated by Congress; it evolved out of the hearts of people who care."

My involvement with hospice care happened in much the same way. Medical science can only do so much and no matter how hard we physicians try, treatments fail and patients die. When these moments come, anything that will help make the coming of death easier for both patient and the family becomes a gift.

I learned everything I know about hospice care firstly from Dame Cicely Saunders and then from many experts in the care of the terminally ill who have led the modern hospice movement in the world as we know it today. My role started at the Georgetown University Hospital, a Catholic hospital, in Washington, D.C. I was training in medical oncology from 1976 to 1980 and worked at the development of the Georgetown University Hospital/Blue Cross/Blue Shield/Washington Home Pilot Project on Hospice Care. This led to the founding of Hospice of Northern Virginia in Arlington County in 1978, where I lived with my children at the time. From there, I became the first executive director of the National Hospice Organization from 1980 to 1983.

This sequence of events prompted many friends and acquaintances over the years to ask have I written a book. The question was probably motivated by the fact that I was there from the beginning and the interest is more for historical facts than anything else. Many important writers and hospice experts have written on the many aspects of hospice care, and I felt that the public has all the books it needs to learn everything about the care of the terminally ill.

Then I had a small episode in the intensive care unit in a local hospital in Alabang, in the Philippines. I thought I was going to die, but I did not die. Instead I experienced a little of what dying patients go through as they come to the end of life-the loneliness and the need to have loved ones near them to hold their hands and say I love you.

When I was discharged home, I wrote a little on this experience. And then memories of the past flooded my mind and I continued to write. There was no thought of organization or of the technical details that I am sure experienced writers pay attention to when they produce a book. I wrote on topics as they came and when I could not think of any more, I stopped. When people asked me if I had written a book or if I was planning to write one, deep in my heart I knew that if God wanted me to write a book, He would tell me. One day my spiritual director asked me the same question: "Have you written a book on your hospice experience?" I said no. She said: "You should write a book. And this is your apostolic assignment."

The ICU episode helped me respond to the assignment, but without my knowing it. God does write with crooked lines sometimes.

Josefina B. Magno MD
19 March 1999

CHRONOLOGY

- December 28, 1919-Born in San Fernando, Pampanga, Philippines; the second child of Felix Bonifacio Bautista, a lawyer, and Florencia Hernandez, convent-bred and, like Felix, from an upper middle class family
- June 1, 1925-Enrolled in grade one at the Assumption Academy, run by Benedictine nuns in San Fernando
- December 8, 1927-Received First Holy Communion in the parish church
- March 1928-Graduated from primary school as valedictorian, Assumption Academy
- March 1931-Graduated from elementary school as valedictorian, Assumption Academy
- 29 November 1933-Death of mother Florencia H. Bautista, age 42, cerebral hemorrhage
- March 1935-Graduated from high school with first honors, Assumption Academy.
- June 1935-Enrolled for pre-medicine at the University of Santo Tomas in Manila and lived in a dormitory run by nuns.
- March 1937-Graduated from pre-medicine, valedictorian of both the girls' and boys' classes and earned a full scholarship for the college of medicine, University of Santo Tomas
- June 1937-Enrolled in the college of medicine, along with 250 other students
- 8 December 1941-Bombing of Pearl Harbor, the start of World War II
- January 1942-Classes suspended. Family moved to barrio in Pampanga to hide from Japanese invaders May 1942-Returned to Manila to resume medical school at the University of Santo Tomas. Classes held in various hospitals in the city

- September 1943-Graduation from medical school, *magna cum laude*, University of Santo Tomas; Cesar Magno also in the same graduating class from medical school
- November 1943-Took medical board examinations February 1944-Ranked fifth in medical board examinations
- 29 March 1944-Married Cesar Magno, classmate and fellow physician, in San Marcelino Church, Manila, with reception at the Jai Alai, rode decorated horse-drawn calesa to church and reception because all cars were on embargo
- April 1944-Together with Cesar, started to practice medicine in Barrio Calaba in San Isidro, Nueva Ecija, while living in mother-in-law's house
- July 1944-Transferred to first own home, a big rented house in San Isidro town, continued to practice medicine and run a drugstore
- January 1945-Family (father, stepmother, siblings and spouses) evacuated to San Isidro, Nueva Ecija, for safety, food security and togetherness
- 20 April 1945-First son born in San Isidro and named Joselito after Saint Joseph
- 4 August 1946-Second son born in Manila and named Vicente after St. Vincent de Paul
- January 1947-Moved to Tuguegarao in Cagayan, the northernmost province of the Philippines, to farm the huge tract of land owned by Felix B. Bautista which he acquired in his law practice; lived in a nipa house and set up medical practice as well as a drugstore
- 8 June 1947-Third son born in Tuguegarao and named Cesar, Jr.
- July 1947-Father developed brain tumor, accompanied him for surgery at Johns Hopkins Hospital, Baltimore
- September 1947-With Cesar, took post-graduate training in internal medicine at New York University Hospital
- May 1949-Cesar Magno diagnosed with melanoma on right eyelid and radical surgery deprived him of right eye
- July 1949-Finished post-graduate training and returned with Cesar to Manila
- 7 August 1949-Fourth son born in Tuguegarao and named Mario

CHRONOLOGY   xix

- January 1950-Moved into beautiful house built by Cesar in Tuguegarao, because he had decided to be a full-time farmer and businessman so he could better provide for family in the event that he would not live long
- 20 July 1950-Death of father Felix B. Bautista, age 60, complication of brain surgery
- 19 March 1951-Only daughter born on the feast day of Saint Joseph, obviously his special gift, and named Maria Josefina (Nanette)
- 14 February 1953-Fifth son born on Valentine's Day and named Carlo Valentin
- 28 September 1954-Sixth son born and named Manolo
- June 1955-Cesar Magno diagnosed with metastatic melanoma in lungs and spine
- July 1955-Took Cesar to Sloan Kettering Memorial Center in New York in desperate attempt to find cure; stayed for three months without relief; went to shrine of Our Lady in Lourdes asking for a miracle
- 7 November 1955-Returned to Manila
- 22 December 1955-Death of husband Cesar Magno, age 38, cancer
- April 1958-Moved family to Manila so that the boys could study in Ateneo and Nanette in Maryknoll
- March 1959-Took first job as special assistant to Dr. Paulino Garcia, chairman of the National Science Development Board (NSDB), a new government agency created by the Science Act of 1958
- November 1961-Became special assistant to the vice president for development of the Ateneo de Manila University, Dr. Paulino 's new job after he left NSDB
- November 1964-Re-joined government service as assistant to newly appointed Secretary of Health Dr. Paulino Garcia
- February 1969-Resigned government position to go to the United States to rest for one year
- May 1969 Arrived in the US with daughter Nanette and niece Lorni
- June-August 1969-Took special courses in family counseling at Georgetown University and the Washington School of Psychiatry

- January 1970-Began work at George Washington University Hospital as community medical coordinator of the rehabilitation project of the Department of Health, Education and Welfare (HEW)
- May 1971-Assigned to the office of the Secretary of Health Education and Welfare with offices in downtown Washington, D.C. July 1972-Radical mastectomy after diagnosis of breast cancer; had five weeks of radiation treatment
- July 1975-Moved to Georgetown University Hospital to be one of its four fellows in medical oncology
- July-December 1976-Went to St. Christopher's Hospice in London to learn about hospice care; also took courses in palliative care in Oxford, Harvard and Royal Victoria Hospital, Montreal
- January 1977 With the staunch support of Rev. Timothy Healy, S.J., president of Georgetown University, started pilot project on hospice by working to link together the medical faculty of Georgetown University, funding from Blue Cross/Blue Shield and the facilities and nursing staff of the Washington Home for Incurables
- June 1977-Inaugurated the six-bed facilities of Georgetown University/Blue Cross/Blue Shield/Washington Pilot Project on Hospice Care
- December 1977 With friends Dorothy Garrett and Pat Pastore, organized the community-based Hospice of Northern Virginia
- 19 March 1978-Inaugurated Hospice of Northern Virginia and assumed responsibility as its medical director concurrent with responsibility as medical director of the pilot project on hospice care in Georgetown
- 7 November 1978-On this day, formally launched hospice care in the US with the first annual meeting of the National Hospice Organization, serving as its first program director. Senator Edward Kennedy was the keynote speaker.
- July 1980-Became the first executive director of the National Hospice Organization (NHO). The number of hospice programs in the US grew from a handful to 1200 within three years:
- October 1981-Became an American citizen
- September 1983-Became director of hospice studies at the Lombardi Cancer Center at Georgetown; resigned as executive director of NHO

- October 1983-Established the International Hospice Institute, based in Georgetown University, to involve and train physicians in the delivery of hospice care
- 19 March 1984-Presided at first board meeting of the International Hospice Institute on this date which is considered as its birth date
- September 1984-Moved to Michigan to help establish Hospice of Southeastern Michigan
- July 1985-First annual symposium for the training of physicians in hospice care
- February 1987-Joined Henry Ford Hospital to found the hospice program for the Henry Ford Health System
- July 1988-Founded the Academy of Hospice Physicians
- July 1989 Asked by the World Health Organization (WHO) to help bring the concept of hospice care to developing countries of the world and IHI expanded its mission to include this
- 2 March 1992-Death of son Mario Bautista Magno, age 42, cancer
- September 1994-To spend more time in the Philippines in order to introduce the hospice concept of care, resigned from job as director of hospice education, research and development at Henry Ford Health System- Josefina B Magno Endowed Chair in Hospice established – one of the first of it's kind in the country
- July 1995-The Academy of Hospice Physicians separated itself from IHI and named itself the American Academy of Palliative Care
- July 1996-The International Hospice Institute became the International Hospice Institute and College and its membership and board of directors became truly international
- July 1997-Created a management committee to run the affairs of IHIC in order to spend more time in the Philippines
- November 1997-Prolonged stay in the Philippines to be with two sisters who had cancer and to do more work on hospice development
- July 1998-Appointed president emeritus of International Hospice Institute and College
- December 1998-Returned to the Philippines to do more work on hospice, principally to develop model hospice programs that can be replicated

all over the country and in other developing nations, and to develop a training course on hospice care for volunteers and caregivers which can be replicated in many communities so that the dying can be given the appropriate care they need while a formal hospice program still has to be established

1

What is hospice

In any language, the saddest words are when the doctor says to a patient: "There is nothing more that I can do. All the treatments available have been tried and they have all failed, and there just is nothing more that can be done."

When this moment comes, there are two options left for the patient. He can resort to experimental drugs in one last desperate attempt to get cured, usually with great suffering because of the side effects and at great financial cost that can leave the family destitute. Or he can do nothing and just die, usually in pain, without medical attention.

But Sir William Osier, a great internist, has redefined good medicine as follows: "Good medicine *cures* sometimes, it *palliates* often, but it *comforts* always." With this definition, no physician should ever say to a patient that there is nothing more that he can do. While there is nothing more that can be done to cure, there is no limit to what can be done to make the patient as comfortable as possible, and to provide him and the members of his family with the comfort and the support that they need at this stressful time.

In effect, this is what hospice care is. When cure of disease is no longer possible, the focus of the treatment should shift from *curing* to *caring*. The physician can now say to the patient: "I can no longer cure you, but I will continue to care for you."

Hospice suggests that the last days or weeks or months of a patient's life can be and should be the most meaningful part of that life. It is the time when goodbyes can be said, material things put in order, broken relationships mended, forgiveness extended or received, and when love, which may never have been expressed before, can finally be expressed. In the words of Dr. Elisabeth Kubler-Ross in her famous book, *On Death and Dying,* "a human being should be alive until he dies."

How does hospice accomplish all these? Hospice care addresses the needs and the problems that are unique to the dying patient. There are many studies on the subject in the literature, but I always go back to an unpublished study by Bishop Edward Crowther in the early 1970's. Dr. Crowther was a bishop in the Episcopal Church in Southern California, and he did a doctoral dissertation entitled, "Care versus Cure in Terminal Illness." He interviewed hundreds of dying patients in the United States and in England and he asked them what their problems and needs were. He summarized their answers under three categories: *pain, loneliness, and loss of control.*

Pain in the terminally ill serves no useful purpose from the purely physical standpoint. In the patient who is going to get well, the pain helps the physicians make a diagnosis of disease, and it is important not to relieve it. But in the dying patient where a diagnosis had been made and all treatments had been tried without success, the pain as a symptom is "senseless, meaningless and unnecessary", in the words of Dame Cicely Saunders, foundress of the modern hospice movement. Therefore, it is cruel and inhumane to allow that patient to die sometimes screaming because of excruciating pain.

Hospice care has shown that pain in the dying can be controlled. It is a question of identifying the cause of the pain and then using the correct drug or combination of drugs in the right amount and in the most effective way of administering them. A study made at St. Christopher's Hospice in England showed that out of 10,000 cancer patients provided with hospice care, only in 5% of these patients was the pain not fully controlled. At best, it was reduced to a level that was bearable.

In the Christian tradition, pain can be seen as an invitation to participate in Christ's redemptive sacrifice. It can have a redemptive meaning for the sins of others, the purification of their souls, and a great treasure, which can draw tremendous blessings from God. I have had patients who asked me if they can "keep their pain for a while so they can offer it for the intentions of someone they love." Their pain had become an opportunity to make one last act of love and thus attain great meaning for themselves.

But pain can also be the cause for self-absorption, and at times even despair and a revolt against God. It is one of the mysteries of human life and through it, man can also recognize his limitations, his powerlessness and his finiteness and thus attain maturity. It can also help him discern in his life what is not essential and just focus on those things which really matter. Sometimes it is the pain that can lead to conversion, to a search for something which often can lead a man back to God. It is this phenomenon that might explain why some preliminary studies have shown that in some cases, the greatest spiritual development in terminally ill patients, happens during the last days or weeks of life.

Loneliness is a big problem in the dying, and the pain of loneliness can be as excruciating as physical pain. Unfortunately, the pain of loneliness cannot be alleviated with drugs or medication; it can be alleviated only with a great deal of loving care and attention. That is why in hospice care, the family is enabled to get involved with the care of the loved one.

Why do families send patients to a hospital? Because they do not know what to do. If the family can be made to understand what is going on and how to address problems that may arise, it will help them be part of the dying process. This helps both the patient in his needs and the family in their grieving later on.

Another way by which the pain of loneliness in the dying is alleviated is by the use of volunteers. In my mind, volunteers are the heart of hospice. They do all the wonderful things they do to help the patient and the family, not because they are paid to do them, but because they want to do them.

Doctors and nurses and the other professionals on the hospice team may be caring individuals, but patients and families know they are doing a job and they are getting paid to do it. There is a difference. It is the volunteers who make the loving and the caring part of hospice so much more visible and tangible. In other words, the volunteers can make *love* something real to both patients and families. Because God is Love, the volunteers bring God to the work they are doing.

The third problem that the dying patient encounters is loss of control. Every human being, regardless of status in life, is in control of things that affect him: what food to eat, what clothes to wear, what job to take. When an individual reaches the end of his life, it becomes even more important that he should matter, that he is not a number on a chart or a diagnosis down the hall. That is why in hospice care, the patient is allowed to make the decisions that he is capable of making: is the pain medication working, is it too much, is it too little? If he says he wants breakfast at 3:00 in the morning and he wants an omelet, why should he be asked to wait for 7:00 and be given oatmeal?

In addition to addressing the needs and the problems that are unique to the dying patient, hospice care has special features that are usually not found in conventional medical care.

In hospice, the unit of care is both patient and the members of the family. This implies a bereavement follow-up after the patient dies to help the family through the first death anniversary and to ensure that the grieving process is normal.

Hospice recognizes that a human being is not just a physical body that can have disease, but is a composite of the physical, the social, the psychological, and the spiritual. That is why hospice care is provided by a hospice team, which consists of physicians, nurses, social workers, clergy and volunteers, to ensure that all the problems that pertain to all the aspects of the patient's being are addressed competently and effectively.

Hospice care is provided in the patient's own home because many studies have shown that patients prefer to die at home, surrounded by familiar things and the people they love.

Many books have been written on the details of how hospice care is provided to terminally ill patients. What is most important is to keep in mind that hospice *is not a* place. It is a *concept of care* to help the dying, and it can be provided in the home, in a hospital, in a nursing home, or wherever the patient is.

I learned about the hospice concept in 1976. Since then up to the present, I have spent all my working hours to introduce it and make it grow in America and, in the 90s, to bring it to Third World countries, including the Philippines.

2
The journey begins

I was born in the Philippines, a country which was colonized by Spain four centuries earlier, and thus became the only Catholic country in the Far East. Even today, 85% of the Philippine population is Roman Catholic.

My parents were of course Catholic. All nine of us children were baptized in the Roman Catholic Church. My mother was a deeply religious woman who was very devoted to Saint Joseph. My earliest recollection of her was that she went to Mass on Sunday wearing the *habito* of Saint Joseph, which consisted of a green skirt and a yellow *camisa, a* blouse of the time, with a yellow and green cord tied around her waist. When she died at the young age of 42 of cerebral hemorrhage, she lay in her coffin wearing the same clothes as a token of devotion to her favorite saint.

My father was a lawyer-an erudite man who was also a writer and a poet. He was the first man in his province to earn a doctorate in law from the University of Washington in Seattle. When his first child, a daughter, was born, she was named after his favorite novel heroine, Alma (meaning soul). When I was born a year afterwards, obviously it was my mother's turn to choose the name of the child, because I was baptized Josefina in honor of Saint Joseph. There had to be a compromise of some sort in the naming process. My nickname became "Nenette", again after one of my father's favorite French fiction heroines. The seven children that followed were named after grandmothers, grandfathers, or after my father, my mother, or a saint who was popular at the time.

We lived in San Fernando, a town which was the capital of the province, Pampanga. It was named after King Ferdinand of Spain, and the name persists up to the present. Our house was about a kilometer away from the town plaza where the Catholic church was, as were the other important establishments of the era. Before entering the town, we had to go over a concrete bridge which spanned the Pampanga River.

I was probably five years old when my parents decided it was time for me to go to kindergarten. I never found out why, because my older sister did not have to go. I do not remember much of what went on in school except for a sandbox where we all played. I do remember getting into fights with some of the boys.

My sisters still tease me about how I ran after a boy at school for a long distance so I could punch him on the nose. The school building was made of concrete and it was located on the left side of the bridge on the way to the town.

The following year, the Benedictine nuns moved into our town and opened the first Catholic school in the province. It was called Assumption Academy, probably because the image on the main altar of our church was a beautiful statue of the Assumption of our Blessed Mother into heaven. All of us who were eligible to go to school were enrolled with the nuns and this became our formal education and our introduction to the Catholic faith.

The sister who was born after me was named-Nicolasa after my mother's mother. We call her Noli to compensate for what we all thought was a terrible name. Then came a boy, named Felix, Jr., after my father. Then another girl, Lucila, named after St. Lucy; then another girl, Libertad (freedom) because she was born on July 4, the Independence Day of the US; then another boy, Apolonio, after my father's father; then another girl, Teresita, named after St. Therese of Lisieux; and then the youngest daughter, Florencia, named after my mother. We were seven girls and two boys.

All my siblings, in one way or another, influenced my growing up. Among all of them, however, it was Noli, the third child, who was my soul mate and companion. I remember how the two of us, ages 11 and 12, woke up early each day and walked one kilometer to go to daily Mass. Was it the nuns' influence? Or was it a special grace of God? We do not know, but we continued to do this all through college and afterwards.

My mother was always in poor health and this may have been one of the reasons why Noli and I went to daily Mass-to pray for her recovery. Another reason was the fact that my father, being a prominent civic leader and politician was a Freemason, and it was only much later that I understood that during those times, for any one to succeed in the profession of law, a man had to belong to that elite organization. The nuns never failed to remind us that all Freemasons were going straight to hell, and we wanted to save the soul of Papa by praying very hard for him.

I was always a very good student and there was a strict German nun who probably drew the best out of me. Her name was Sister Florencia. During those days, one teacher handled all the subjects for the class, so she started with religion, the first subject of the day. We were given assignments, which included the study of a certain parable from the New Testament for that day. We were called to discuss the parable in our own words and strictly told never to memorize it. When my turn came, I always recited the assigned parable word for word, and I was scolded for it. I did not memorize, but I seem to have a photographic memory and I could not help it.

At school, we had the Sodality of Our Lady as well as the Legion of Mary. In the Sodality, we had to go through various levels before becoming a member and the criteria included good behavior at all times and always acting like a lady, as befits a daughter of Mary. We said the Office of Our Lady every Friday afternoon.

Noli and I continued to go to Mass every day. We prayed for Mama to get well, but God called her home when I was in second year high school and Noli was in first year.

Life was very difficult after she died, but it brought all of us, nine children, very close to one another. We were all in black, and when we went to Sunday Mass, we all knelt in one pew. People were very sorry for us.

My father did not go to Mass except on Christmas Eve, so we all prayed for his conversion. Our prayers were answered. In the last year of his life, he met a Jesuit priest whom he liked very much. One day he surprised all of us by going to Mass with us and receiving Holy Communion. He had been converted in answer to our prayers.

At the Assumption Academy, I had literally grown up under the tutelage of the nuns, straight from grade one up to graduation from high school. It had been a very happy time in my life. I was almost always at the top of my class, was editor-in-chief of our high school paper and president of the student council. I graduated first honors, not valedictorian nor even salutatorian, but that was acceptable at the time. Since my mother died, my father single-handedly brought up all of us nine siblings.

After high school graduation, the logical question to ask was: what degree will I pursue in college which would be meaningful for the future? At that time in the Philippines, women went to college, not really in order to have a career, but because it was the right thing to do. Every son or daughter should have a college diploma to hang on the walls of the living room of the family home. That was the epitome of a "successful" family.

My older sister, Alma, had chosen to be a teacher so she went to the college of education of the University of Santo Tomas. There was no question that the school had to be a Catholic school and would have a strict separation between the boys' and the girls' classes. She was one year ahead of me in college.

My father asked me what I would like to study in college. He was one of those intelligent parents who knew that it was important that the child be allowed to choose his or her path to higher education, so he gave me the choice. At that point in my life, I really had no great ambitions about the future, but I loved to cook and to sew. I do not understand this kind of predilection for the home arts because when I was in fourth grade, I got the only almost failing grade in my whole life. Amidst all the Excellent and Outstanding marks, there was this terrible grade of "Just Passing" because I could not finish my project. It was a piano cover with an ambitious border in cross-stitch of a grape vine, with dark violet grapes and green leaves. I am sure my good mother had to stay up late many nights to help me finish it and to save me from a failing grade.

I thought about what I would like to study in college when my father asked. The only thing I really wanted to do was to study home economics. He agreed and plans were made accordingly. Now in the Philippines, there are extended families with many aunts and uncles and cousins, all of whom get involved with what the families are doing. I am sure it was this situation which caused my father to think things over. Everyone was obviously telling him: how can he allow me to waste my talents by taking up home economics? One day, he had a talk with me which in effect said: "You can learn how to cook and sew without going to college. Can you think of something else that you might want to study?"

I really did not have anything else in mind. I did not have any burning ambition to become something other than a housewife who could cook and sew. But I loved going to school and I could easily spend my whole life studying, so I thought of the longest course that anyone could take, medicine. So I said: "May I go to medical school?" My father was ecstatic.

I enrolled in pre-medicine at the University of Santo Tomas. In high school, I had sort of been one of the favored students because of my high grades and the other extracurricular activities I was involved in. Besides, all my classmates had been my friends for many years, and the nuns and the other teachers had all been familiar faces who were always there to teach and to guide. And being in San Fernando, Pampanga, was a far cry from being in a big city like Manila, with its busy roads and constant noise.

My first day in class was a most traumatic experience. My classmates came from all parts of the Philippines and many of them spoke strange dialects. They also strutted around, seeming to know everything. I felt like a total stranger who did not belong.

I went back to the dormitory (the Immaculate Conception Dormitory which was across the street from the University of Santo Tomas) and I cried and cried. I called my father on the phone and told him I wanted to go home and I did not want to go to college.

He was very patient and understanding and he told me to just give college a try for three to five days. If things did not change, he would come to get me and bring me home. This offer comforted me and I went back to class knowing that I had only to be brave for a few days and then I would be back home.

Those three days changed my attitude. I found out that these strangers could actually be nice people. They did not really know all the answers and they were as frightened and as homesick as I was. Before I knew it, I was enjoying myself and having the time of my life. My wise father knew how to deal with me.

My sister Alma and I stayed in the dormitory run by the Religious of the Virgin Mary (RVM). It had a chapel where the Mass was offered daily. Since the chapel was located across the room where my sister and I were assigned together with six other girls, it was very convenient for me to make visits to the Blessed Sacrament frequently. I studied very hard, and I prayed a lot. I finished pre-med as class valedictorian of both the girls' and the boys' classes and I was given a full scholarship to medicine school proper.

During my days in pre-med, I chose to wear the *habito* of Saint Joseph just the way my saintly mother did. It was a dark green dress with a yellow and green cord around the waist. The cord ended with seven yellow and green balls made of yarn by way of a tassel. It must have looked weird but I wanted to do this from the depth of my heart. I wore the green dress every day all through medical school except when we were obliged to wear the white uniform of a medical student. For many years afterwards, I continued to wear green for Saint Joseph. Was this devotion to Saint Joseph which at the time seemed so external what eventually led me to know his foster son Jesus? We never fully know the mysterious ways of God.

For medicine proper, the University of Santo Tomas moved us to another part of the city, in Intramuros, the ancient walled city. Even during this time, I stayed in a convent, again of the RVM Sisters. There was a chapel, there was Mass every day, and I made frequent visits to the Blessed Sacrament. The university obliged us to make a yearly retreat, and we had subjects in religion. The university was run by the Dominicans (Order of Preachers) so we observed many religious holy days and went in processions in honor of Our Lady of the Rosary and Christ the King. Without my knowing it, I was receiving spiritual formation.

In my last year of medical school, the second World War disrupted everything and my family, as did so many others, had to flee into the remotest barrios of the province to escape the brutality of the Japanese invaders. It took almost three years before formal classes could be resumed, but our medical training took place in various hospitals in Manila and I did finish medical school, took the board exams and immediately afterwards married Cesar Magno, my classmate and fellow doctor. We moved to his province, went into private practice, and had seven children, one after another, six boys and one girl, in the course of eleven years. It was a very happy marriage. I continued to go to daily Mass, said the Rosary with Cesar every day, and enrolled the children in a Catholic school.

3

The man I married

When I was a medical student in the University of Santo Tomas, the laboratories were on the third floor, the uppermost floor: The tables faced an open patio, which is typical of Spanish architecture. Students walking through this patio saw what was going on in the laboratories and who was working with the test tubes and peering into the microscopes.

I had always been a very good and conscientious student as a young girl and this did not change in medical school. In the Immaculate Conception Dormitory, I was with three classmates, Felicidad, Beatriz and Remedios, who were my constant companions. I always wore the dark green *habito* of Saint Joseph. I wore this outfit to school every day. Felicidad was a devotee of Our Lady of Lourdes and she wore a white dress with a blue sash around the waist all the time also. Beatriz was always in black, mourning for her mother who had recently passed away. Remedios was the socialite of the group and she was wearing beautiful dresses all the time.

We must have made a weird combination, all four of us, but times were different then. We were close friends and we studied together and did everything' together. We had fun.

One day I received a phone call. It was a gentleman who said his name was Cesar Magno. He said I did not know him, but that he had been watching me at the laboratories on the third floor and he wanted to meet me. He was in engineering school. He said he was the tall one in the group of three who frequented the third floor. I hung up on him. I was in second year pre-med.

The call started a courtship which lasted for almost seven years. He shifted from engineering to pre-med so he could be closer to me, but that did not impress me at all. He wrote letters every day, he sent flowers, he sent telegrams, he asked if he may visit me, and I said no. He persisted. He came to the dormitory to visit me and I refused to see him. When my friends and I went to the movies, he and his friends went also and he bought balcony tickets for all of us, just so they would have a chance to talk with us. Nothing worked-I still refused to talk to him.

All of this behavior is totally incomprehensible today when after boy meets girl, things go on from there. By second year medicine proper, I had become president of my class and Cesar was president of his own class. It is to be remembered that in the University of Santo Tomas, the girls' entrance into the university buildings was separate from that of the boys. Classes were distinctly not coed. In order to have a chance to be with me, Cesar would organize a boys' class activity such as an excursion or a picnic and invite our girls' class. I refused to attend. There was a formal ball organized by him. All my friends went, but I did not.

My girl friends were all rooting for him. After all, he was the handsomest and the best-dressed student in that batch of future physicians. He was a class leader. He had money to spend. What more did I want? I do not know. He had told everyone that the moment he had laid eyes on me on the third floor of the university, he had decided that I would be the mother of his children. Girls were after him, but no one succeeded in changing his mind about me.

Later on, I heard that he used to hope that I would change my green dress because he did not understand what the *habito* was for. Yet he continued to be in love with me in spite of the fact that I was not a fashion model. The daily letters, the telegrams, the flowers continued to come and I still refused to see him or talk to him.

At third year medicine proper, I fell in love with a fourth year medical student. He seemed such a trophy-good-looking, suave, fluent in English and Spanish, from a good school, part of the drama group. He had started his courtship by going to my father and asking permission to court his daughter, a gesture that impressed both my father and myself. Since I was one of the popular students at the time, and because the whole campus was aware of the tireless efforts that Cesar had exerted for many years to win my favor, this development was not left unnoticed. Everyone watched, wondering how Cesar would react.

How did he react? He wrote me a letter saying that he loved me very much and all he wanted was for me to be happy with whomever I married. In order to enable me to find that out, he said he would stop writing to me for one whole year. He would stay completely out of the picture so that I would have all the time in the world to find out what I wanted. He kept his word. The letters and the telegrams and the flowers stopped coming, and he completely disappeared from my universe. Then World War II broke out. Classes were suspended. My family and I evacuated to the remotest barrio of our province to escape from the Japanese invaders. The place where we hid was accessible only by boat.

By this time, the one year that Cesar had given himself to stay out of my life had come to an end. He lived in Nueva Ecija, a province which was many hours away from my own. But, one day, riding on a small boat and bringing mangoes, he showed up at our place of evacuation. He had traveled for many hours by a horse-drawn cart looking for the town we were in and then hired a boat to find us, and there he was.

Shortly afterwards, when the danger from the Japanese had ended, my family went back to our home in town. There he sent me a letter saying that since the one year he had promised not to bother me had finished, he wanted me to know that he still loved me and he wanted to marry me.

It was October 1943. I went to my mother's grave and asked her to tell me what to do. I prayed to Saint Joseph and asked for his guidance. By November that year, shortly after All Souls' Day, I knew the answer. The other man had come to visit one day traveling all the way from Manila to my hometown, and I told him that I had found out that I was not in love with him after all, and therefore I could not marry him.

Cesar began to come to our house regularly. Within four months, on March 29, 1944, we got married in a beautiful ceremony in Manila. In spite of the war, there still was a prominent couturier who made my wedding gown; I had orange blossoms on my hair; I had white orchids in my wedding bouquet. We had an elegant reception in Jai-alai, a much sought-after venue for wedding parties for those who could afford it.

Cesar's father had died when he was one year old; his mother was a rich lady who could neither read nor write, but she had all the figures and numbers she needed in her mind. She gave us some money telling us we could do what we wanted with it: spend it all on the wedding or keep it for our future. Cesar said we should spend it all on the wedding and we did.

It was 1944 and the times were uncertain. Cesar decided that we would be better off in the province because we would at least have rice and food even if we did not have any money. His mother lived in a huge house which certainly could accommodate us.

My mother-in-law asked me if I knew how to cook and of course I said no, I did not know how. She asked me if I knew how to clean fish, and again I said no. So she patiently asked me to sit beside her. She took my right hand, put it on the fish that she was cleaning and then gave me step by step instructions on what to do. It was all new to me, but soon Cesar announced to his family that he did not like the smell of garlic on my hands, so I should not be asked to touch garlic. That probably was the end to my role in his mother's kitchen. I did love all the members of his family, and they loved me very much. I still have the fondest memories of my mother-in-law, and all his brothers and his only sister, all my in-laws. I felt very fortunate in marrying into this wonderful family. About three months after our wedding and when we were living in his mother's house, Cesar decided one day that we should move into town, San Isidro, so we could start private practice. We found a house to rent. The advantage in small towns in the Philippines is the fact that everyone is practically related to everyone, and of course, everyone knew everybody else. The house we rented was a big one. On the large ground floor, we opened a small drugstore and started practicing general medicine.

I graduated with honors from medical school, but Cesar was a naturally good clinician and surgeon. He had tremendous compassion for his patients, and an integrity, which enabled him to do for them only the best that he could offer without exploiting their trust. Patients in their ignorance tended to equate an injection of something with a miracle cure, so they would beg for an injection even if they did not need one. It would be an opportunity to charge them more and make a profit, but Cesar patiently explained why he was not giving an injection until they fully understood. His reputation as a good and caring physician soon spread far and wide and he became a successful practitioner.

One day in October 1944, when I was three months pregnant with our first child, Cesar said suddenly: "We have to save Papa (my father) and your family and bring them here to San Isidro. The Japanese are retreating and no one knows what they might do." My family was then living in Manila but had evacuated to Polo, Bulacan, to live with the cousins of my stepmother. The Japanese had begun to kill civilians left and right. Over the objections of my mother-in-law who feared for our safety, Cesar prepared his horse-drawn cart, placed a sack of rice under the seat and we took off. There were no motor vehicles on the road because the Japanese had commandeered every single one they could lay hands on. After two days of traveling, we reached my father's home in Manila only to find out that my family had moved to Polo, Bulacan.

We proceeded to Polo, passing interminable Japanese checkpoints. We had to bow and show all kinds of identification papers, but we found the house where my family was staying. We were offered a meal, a thin rice porridge and that was it. Cesar told my father that we had to leave that same night because he had to be back in San Isidro in two days.

My father had an old Fiat car which fortunately the Japanese had not seen, so my father, my stepmother, my brother and his wife, and my two sisters piled into the car and we all took off for San Isidro, Nueva Ecija. I am sure it was a very difficult journey, and I do not even remember the details. What is unforgettable, however, was the fact that on the following morning after we had all left, the Japanese came and took all the men in the house and shot them in the town plaza.

What made my husband think of rescuing my family? In the absence of communication, we did not even know that they were in danger. Were the seven years of hard labor, during which he had tried everything to make me fall in love with him, part of God's loving plan to save my whole family from a terrible fate in the hands of the Japanese? In retrospect, it is very easy to see God's hand in all the things that happened, but while all these were going on we did not really understand the miracles that were happening. Cesar and I settled my family in the house we were then renting, and we moved to a smaller house two doors away. In February 1945, liberation came and things were good. I had my first baby, a son whom we named Jose after St. Joseph. Then my father had a brilliant idea. As a lawyer, he had accumulated some 13,000 hectares of land (26,000 acres) in the province of Cagayan in the northern part of the Philippines. Since he had been a lawyer all his life, he had absolutely no idea what farming was all about. On the other hand, my husband came from a rice producing family and he knew all about rice production. My father said to him: "Why don't you look at the land in Cagayan and see if you might want to do something about it?" My husband went, and he decided we would move to Cagayan and, in addition to being a doctor, he would farm the land.

My father's younger brother, Melquiades, had already moved to Cagayan two years earlier to go into farming. He had built a house out of bamboo and nipa thatch in the commercial center of the town, Tuguegarao. Because his wife was a pharmacist, he opened a drugstore in front of the house, called Doctors' Drug. The house, square in shape with a porch at one end, was then divided into four rooms. Two rooms were on one side and two on the other with a corridor in between. My uncle and his family occupied one room, my husband and I occupied another, and then my brother-in-law and my sister also moved to Tuguegarao and occupied another room. I think all the housemaids were piled into the remaining room. The lower part of the house was the dining room with a long table where we all had our meals, and at its end at the back was the kitchen.

My husband's office for his practice was part of the drugstore, so in no time at all, we were settled in our new home. Considering how big and comfortable the houses were where we had lived in San Isidro, I cannot now imagine how we managed in the cramped quarters. All I remember is how very happy we all were.

I was having a baby every 15-18 months because Cesar and I decided we wanted to have 12 children. Because of pregnancy and caring for our babies, I really did not practice medicine, although I did help in the drugstore.

Cesar measured off 300 hectares of my father's huge land and started farming. It was an exciting time for us. The farmers in Cagayan were very primitive: their seeds were poor, their techniques obsolete, and they were always at the mercy of loan sharks who took advantage of their poverty and ignorance to lend them money at usurious rates.

My husband was probably a missionary at heart. Before too long, he had started on a campaign to introduce new varieties of rice, taught the farmers newer methods of planting, harvesting and cultivating the land, and even introduced the concept of cooperatives to liberate them from loan sharks. He established a dealership in agricultural machinery so he and the farmers could buy these machines at a discount.

In the meantime, his practice of medicine continued to grow. After we had our third child, Cesar and I went to the United States, first to bring my father to Johns Hopkins University Hospital for brain tumor surgery. The children were left in the care of my sister-in-law in the ancestral home in Nueva Ecija. When my father returned home after the surgery, Cesar and I moved to New York to pursue further training in internal medicine. We went back to the Philippines after one year so I could give birth to our fourth son, Mario, who was conceived in the U.S.

Before we left New York, I asked Cesar to consult specialists about a black stain in the inner canthus of his right eye. He had had it for twenty years, he said, and all the specialists in Manila said it was nothing to worry about. But I insisted, saying that I would feel better if the experts in New York would look at it. They did and the diagnosis was melanoma. The treatment? The doctors recommended the removal not only of the eyeball, but also of everything in the socket of the right eye.

Cesar faced a very hard decision. Here was a man, 31 years old, very handsome, very successful with a very bright future ahead of him. How could he agree to be deformed? I convinced him that I would be more at peace if he had the surgery. And so he did. The surgery was done by Dr. Ramon Castroviejo, at that time, the most famous cancer surgeon in the United States.

We came home at the end of July of that year, 1949. Cesar had a prosthesis to cover the socket where his right eye used to be and he had to wear dark glasses all the time. But life went on. My fourth son, Mario, was born on August 7, 1949.

He was to be the apple of my eye, my spiritual director, and everybody's beloved friend and counselor.

One day Cesar told me: "The diagnosis of melanoma does not guarantee me a long life. If I just depend on my practice, you will not have enough money when I am gone." So he decided to be a gentleman farmer, and relegated the practice of medicine to a part-time occupation.

He plunged into farming with the passion and intensity that was so characteristic of him. He set up a piggery and a poultry farm. He bought a small farm close to the town proper and built a vacation cottage to which we would go at the end of the day. The important thing was that I was with him everywhere he wanted to go. He never went to a party or a movie without me because he said he did not enjoy any of these if I was not with him. Every so often, he would say, let us fly to Manila so we can eat at this restaurant, or have breakfast at that hotel, and we would go: We had many friends.

He built a house for me, which was typical of his good taste. He was not happy with local carpenters, so he had architects and builders and decorators coming all the way from Manila. I remember one thing about the house. The flooring was made exactly the way bowling alleys were made in Manila, hard wood very meticulously installed for a smooth and flawless surface.

In 1951, our only daughter was born. By this time, we had four boys so Cesar told me to give up on having a girl. He said I would probably have ten boys in a row-enough for two basketball teams. I was very pregnant, and it was not yet time for me to have the baby. We were at Mass on March 19, feast of Saint Joseph, when I developed labor pains. Because this baby was going to be the fifth boy, I did not prepare anything in terms of a layette. I had all kinds of blue hand-me-downs for him to wear. And then the baby was born and it was a girl. Everyone started to scream and jump with joy. She was baptized Maria Josefina in honor of Saint Joseph. We called her Nanette and she was the carbon copy of her handsome father.

Two more boys were born after Nanette: Carlo on Valentine's Day in 1953, and Manolo on September 28, 1954: Life went on, and things were good.

One day late in the afternoon, Cesar came back from seeing patients and he complained of pain in his lower back. I quickly diagnosed a slipped disc because he was always riding on a tractor or driving a Jeep over rough terrain. I decided to fly him to Manila, though, for X-rays, just to be sure.

He and I were very optimistic and we never suspected anything to be really wrong. After all, it had been seven years since his surgery for the melanoma and the best doctors in the world had performed the most radical procedure to cure him. And then the radiologist came out with a puzzled look on his face. There was no slipped disc, but what were those cotton ball-looking lesions in portions of his lungs that showed in the X-rays? The truth dawned on us simultaneously: cotton-ball metastasis from the melanoma. It was the end of the world.

The first thing my husband told me was: "Do not tell anyone." And then we proceeded to the company which carried his life insurance and he told the manager: "I am going to die. I do not want you to make things difficult for my wife after I am gone, so let me sign any papers that I need to sign now" And then we went home to my father's house where all of us stayed every time we visited Manila. There he took down his books on medicine and started to read all he could find on metastatic melanoma. He said: "If I can have at least one year, I can provide all the things I want to provide for you and the children."

I cried and cried day and night for three days. I could not stop crying. My eyes got so swollen from crying that I could not see anything unless I pried my eyelids open with my fingers. How could God do this?

My brother Felix was a writer. At that time, he was writing a book with Father John Delaney, S.J., chaplain of the University of the Philippines campus in Diliman, Quezon City. He felt that a visit with Father Delaney would help us so he arranged for a meeting.

As soon as Father Delaney saw me, he asked, "Why are you crying? If you love your husband, you should be happy he is going to see God before you do."

He turned to Cesar and asked him: "Why are you afraid to die?" My husband said: "I am not afraid, Father. I am just worried about what will happen to my wife and our seven little children when I die." Father Delaney said: "When you die, you can take better care of your children because you will be with God and all your prayers will be effective."

I stopped crying and a tremendous peace came over me and my husband. God had spoken to us through this holy priest and everything would be all right.

My husband told me not to bring him to the United States for treatment. He knew what he had was beyond cure of medical science. I said I would like to place that decision in the hands of God. If He wanted us to go, He would make everything easy. If not, He would tell us. In five days I had everything ready-the money, the documents for travel, and the admission into Sloan Kettering Memorial Cancer Center in New York. And so we left, taking our oldest son Jose with us. Cesar said we should take him along because "when I am gone, he will take my place in helping his younger siblings." Jose was ten years old.

Sloan Kettering Cancer Memorial Hospital knew there was no cure for the melanoma. They treated his back pain with cobalt which gave Cesar some relief, but also gave him unceasing nausea and vomiting. He lost a great deal of weight and three months after our arrival in New York, the doctors told me that whatever they could do, the physicians in the Philippines could do just as well. They reminded me that winter is bitter in New York and we would be better off in the Philippines where it is warmer and we have family. We went home via Lourdes to ask for a miracle. On our first day in Lourdes, Cesar ate a huge breakfast for the first time in three months. I had a fleeting hope that our prayers had been answered. But it was a brief respite. The following day, he was weaker. And we flew back home. It was the first week of November 1955. Early in December, he told me: "If I am not going to get well, let us ask God to help me die. I am ready." And I fell to my knees and asked God to do just that.

Cesar died three days before Christmas, very peacefully, in the San Juan de Dios Hospital after receiving the last Sacraments. I was praying inside his oxygen tent that night when he looked at me and then took a last breath and went home to God. I did not shed any tears.

He was 38 years old and I was 36. Our eldest child was ten years old and the youngest was one year old. We buried him beside his mother and his brother in the town where he was born, because I felt that wherever I and his children might be in the future, he would not be alone and his grave would always be cared for.

Cesar had been involved in many businesses, all of which were flourishing. I had been either pregnant or just finished having a baby, so I did not have the time to help in the business and to know what it was all about. There was the big farm, the agricultural machinery dealership, a poultry, a piggery, a trucking business, and a small clinic.

When he died, I found myself looking at all these undertakings not knowing what to do. I went to church at 5:30 in the morning each day to lay all of the problems in God's hands, asking Him to help me. Then I went back home and tackled each and every one of them in the best way I could.

For three years after my husband's death, I did all this in addition to trying to raise seven little children. I did not practice medicine, gradually sold the piggery and the poultry, leased the farm for a fixed amount each year, and turned over the agricultural machinery dealership to a brother-in-law. I kept the trucks, but I built a rice mill to complement what they were doing, hauling rice to and from the farm. And we transferred to Manila for the good schools. I was still wearing black in and outside of the house, because I was in deep mourning for my husband.

At the end of three years, my youngest son was in kindergarten, so I had more time on my hands. And then the Lord made one of His surprising moves which changed my whole life. One of my professors in medicine came unannounced to our house one day, and told me: "You are wasting the talents that God gave you. Why don't you work with me and help out in the government?" The Philippine government had just passed a law mandating the creation of the National Science Development Board and my former professor, Dr. Paulino Garcia, was the chairman, with cabinet rank.

I responded by saying the first of many such statements that characterized my whole career from then on: "May I try the job for six months? I have not worked for any one before and I want to be sure I will know how" - He agreed.

Working for the government as special assistant to the chairman of the National Science Development Board was an entirely new experience for me. Instead of being my own boss, I had to deal with people at all levels. This experience brought its own share of heartache as well as pleasure, but all in all it enriched my life.

4

Crossing the ocean

I remember very clearly when I made the decision as if I did it only a few days or weeks ago. We were then living in Loyola Heights, a suburb of Manila. Our home was directly in front of the Ateneo, the Jesuit high school. I had moved there shortly after Cesar died. He had said that all his six sons should go to school with the Jesuits who, he believed, offered the best education for boys in the country. Moreover, a Jesuit education was the ultimate status symbol for boys as far as girls were concerned.

We were having breakfast that morning in 1969. All of a sudden, out of the blue, the thought came to me: I want to go to the United States for one year just to "bum around," as I was to describe it later. I was not going to work. I wanted to go sightseeing and shopping and give myself the rest that I felt I badly needed.

I had been working for two years as assistant to the secretary of health, Dr. Paulin Garcia. Before that, for eight years, I had worked with him in various capacities, starting at the National Science Development Board and then at the Ateneo de Manila when he became its vice president for development. They were very fulfilling years because Dr. Garcia was one of the country's most respected public officials. He was a man of vision and of great dreams. Consequently much of the hard work fell on me and the other members of his immediate staff.

I had been in the United States three times before but not for pleasure. The first time was when I accompanied my father for brain tumor surgery at the Johns Hopkins Hospital in Baltimore, Maryland. I was then 26 years old, married with two children whom I left behind at home. The second time was when Cesar and I went to New York City for post-graduate training at New York University. The third time was when I took Cesar to Sloan Kettering Memorial Hospital in a desperate attempt to find a cure for his malignant melanoma. This time, fourteen years after that third trip, I looked forward with excitement to go to the States strictly to enjoy myself.

I planned to take Nanette with me. She was 18 and she had a boyfriend. Preparations for the trip included asking my sons for permission to bring her with me, as well as talking to her boyfriend who begged me not to take Nanette. I promised him that if she was absolutely miserable in the States, I would send her home after three months and he agreed to that. My six sons were more philosophical. They understood that a mother just does not leave an 18-year-old daughter behind for one whole year.

The big task was how to tell my boss. By this time, I had become his right as well as left hand. Surprisingly, he fully understood and gave me permission to go to the US for one year. Once the decision was made and preparations were in earnest, suggestions came from family and friends about where we should go. The consensus was that we should base ourselves in Washington, D.C. It is the nation's capital and it is a beautiful city.

My niece, Lorni, the daughter of my eldest sister, had been living with me for several years while she was studying at the University of the Philippines. She was at the breakfast table when I made the announcement that I wanted to bum in the States for a year. I turned to her and asked: "Would you like to come along?" She did but she was almost sure that her father, a strict and conservative physician, would not allow her. Right away I went to the phone, called her father and asked: "May I bring Lorni with me to the US for one year?" With no questions asked, he said yes. Obviously God was working and all potential obstacles and difficulties were removed one by one.

Since the trip was for pleasure, I asked the travel agent to give us three days in Honolulu and three days in San Francisco. Then we set out for Washington, D.C. With two young girls and four huge suitcases, we really looked like visitors from a developing country. But Nanette and Lorni were bright and adventurous. Nothing intimidated them, not even when our hotel reservation was cancelled in Washington because we were two hours late. This was at 6:00 a.m. when the whole city was asleep. At that hour, I called a friend who was living in Washington because she had a job in the World Bank. I explained our predicament to her. With true Filipino hospitality, she asked us to stay in her apartment for the meantime. We took a cab and, by the time we got to her place; she had a chicken dish ready for us. Before she left for work, she briefed us thoroughly on how to look for an apartment and how much taxi fare should be. The girls went to work at once and by noon were ready to choose which place suited our needs. Before the day was over, we moved into an apartment complex on Pennsylvania Avenue, near a Catholic Church, near a bus stop, near a grocery store and near a drugstore. It was a spring day in May 1969.

Five months later, on a beautiful fall day in October, I was walking down Pennsylvania Avenue toward the shopping district when I passed by a building. The sign on it caught my attention: George Washington University Hospital.

We had been in Washington all these five months and neither Nanette nor Lorni nor I had noticed it. We were too busy being tourists and no one had bothered to point out the place to us. All of a sudden, I had the impulse to go into the building, find out what it was all about and see what was going on inside. It must have been the physician in me. People were going in and out in a steady stream and I concluded that they must be patients. I stood in the small lobby and watched.

I then found myself chatting with two men who were also standing in the lobby. One of them wore a doctor's white coat, the other was in a gray suit. I soon found out that the man in a doctor's coat was the chairman of the department of medicine of the George Washington University Hospital; the man in the gray suit was the newly appointed administrator of the rehabilitation program of the hospital.

Obviously God was working on something unbeknownst to the three of us. They began to discuss the rehabilitation project with me, a total stranger from a developing country. I am sure though that I had told them a little about myself, that I was assistant to the secretary of health in my country but that I was only visiting US, as a tourist. Then the chairman asked me: "Would you like to work with us?"

I responded politely that I did not plan on working while I was in the US and that I was returning to the Philippines after a year to practice internal medicine. Besides I was on a tourist visa which precluded taking a job of any kind.

The gentleman in the gray suit said that the hospital could take care of that detail. I continued to make excuses. Then the chairman of medicine said: "If you work with us, your seven children can immediately go to school tuition-free at George Washington University." The tuition benefit was a perk that the university offered to all the physicians on its hospital staff, so it was nothing extraordinary in my case.

The offer of free tuition for all my children in a prestigious university caused me to pause and think. Later on in the day, Nanette said: "Mommy, how can you pass that up?" I called the administrator and asked: "May I try the job for six months? If I like it, I will stay. If I don't or if you are not happy with me, I will leave, without any problem for anyone." He agreed.

A few days later, I was on the job. It was a thoroughly new experience for me. Office practices were very different from my previous job in the Philippines where, as assistant to the secretary of health, I had access to three or four secretaries. In my new job, I had to share one secretary with other staff members. Everyone always had something urgent to be typed, so I learned in a short while how to use the electric typewriter. Typing with two fingers, the way I still do today, I became very efficient in my job.

The rehabilitation project at George Washington University Hospital was a special project under the Department of Health, Education and Welfare (HEW) of the US government. One year after I accepted the job as community medical coordinator, I was assigned to the office of the secretary of health, education and welfare in downtown Washington, D.C., where all the federal offices were located. I had an advantage. My experience of working with the secretary of health in my country enabled me to have a global perspective, a view from the top, instead of just looking at projects from ground level. Seen in this way, it was a very rewarding experience that was to help me in various future work and responsibilities.

One time, my supervisor called me at 2:00 p.m. and asked me to prepare a position paper on end-stage renal disease. He said that the paper was due at 8:00 a.m. the next day. I went to my typewriter and did my best. I submitted the paper before the close of office hours that same day. I did not give it much thought. I figured that something that had to be as rushed as this paper could not be too important.

Several days later, the supervisor called me to say that the paper I submitted was adjudged the best and that it would be the official position of the US government. Thanks be to God in the Holy Spirit who uses us as His instruments.

On another occasion, the office of the secretary needed some information on how HEW conducted research work which resulted in the employment of the handicapped. Again it was my experience in the office of the secretary of health in the Philippines which enabled me to sift through the thick files in the division where I was assigned. I was able to identify several research projects that had indeed resulted in employment opportunities for the disabled and the handicapped. These projects were given prominence in the US, media later on.

In all these, it was obvious that God was preparing me for hospice development many years before without my being aware of it. The six-month trial period which I had given myself on the rehabilitation project eventually became five years.

5

The house on Military Road

An important event happened in connection with my job at George Washington University Hospital which shows how true it is that God never slumbers. He takes care of our needs even without our asking or knowing.

As I had said earlier, my decision to go to the States for one year was impulsive. There had been neither long premeditation nor careful planning for the trip. Definitely I was not going to work. Before we left Manila, I asked my son Jose to remit to me a certain amount of US dollars a month to take care of our expenses. He did it for about five months, then he called to say that the government had begun to restrict dollars leaving the country. "Just so you will know what to do, Mommy," he said.

At that point, I had no choice but to have a conversation with God. He knew that these things were going to happen, but He still allowed us to go to the US. I told Him that I trusted Him and that I was not going to worry about the problem. I did list down, though, the things for which we needed money: rent, food, travel, books and so on. I came up with a total amount and presented it to Him.

Our precarious situation was not in my mind when I impulsively walked into the George Washington University Hospital that beautiful morning in the fall. I was offered a job, I kept refusing it, I insisted that I was going back home and that I did not come to the US to work. God was patient with my silliness and later on I did accept the job. When I did, I asked how much the salary was. When I was told the amount, it was much, much more than the sum of our expenses which I had earlier presented to God. What I did not know was that there would be deductions for taxes, social security, retirement funds and others. When I received my first paycheck, it was the exact amount that I had asked God to take care of.

Truly impressed and thankful for God's providence, I later shared this specific experience at a prayer meeting with about 300 persons present at Catholic University. For many months afterwards, people approached me on the street or at

Catholic University to tell me that my sharing had touched and even saved their lives. Many of them said that they were on the brink of despair but after listening to my story, they were encouraged to pray and to continue trusting in God.

As soon as I accepted the job at George Washington University Hospital, my sons joined us from the Philippines. We transferred from the apartment on Pennsylvania Avenue to a small bungalow in Arlington, Virginia. With only two bedrooms and one bathroom, it was not the most comfortable place to live in.

The lease was for a whole year, and we were happy enough and content. It was all we could afford, and we were willing to continue living in this little home. My children soon made friends who came to visit and share our meals.

When the lease ended, the owners told us that they were selling the property. We had the choice to buy it or to move out. The decision had to be made right away. My children and I had a meeting. The decision was to move to a bigger place. We then started the exhausting process of house hunting. With a limited budget and a relatively big family, it was not easy.

We had only a weekend to find another house and to move in. By this time, we had a second-hand Mustang and we piled into it. We drove round and round Arlington looking for a For Rent sign. We found many signs but the houses were either too small or too big. It was very discouraging.

By Sunday afternoon, we were all exhausted and depressed. My son Mario cheered us up and said: "Let's make one more round, then we can quit."

We did make one more trip around the block, in a manner of speaking, and we ended up on Military Road. It was one of the most expensive areas at that time, with beautiful homes and well-kept gardens and it is close to Washington. We were not really looking but at one of the homes, a young boy was mowing the lawn. He was the classmate of Manny, my youngest son.

We slowed down so Manny could say hello. And then, lo and behold, there was a For Rent sign planted on the front lawn. We had passed by this house at least six times before but we never saw the sign which was in big red letters.

We got out of the car and went in. We looked at one another in amazement. It was perfect for our needs: four bedrooms, three bathrooms, a fully finished basement and family room. With trepidation, I asked the boy: "How much is the rent?" He mentioned an amount then quickly added: "But you can ask my mom to reduce it if it is too much." The price was just right, because it was a gift package that God had prepared for us. Mario said: "Let us pray." In the middle of the empty living room, we knelt down and said a prayer of thanks.

The following day, we moved in. There was a tree in the backyard, birds were singing and the sun was shining. How wonderful are the ways of God.

We had been one year in the house when I had this thought: "Wouldn't it be wonderful if we could buy this house?" It was an absurd thought, of course, but I whispered it to God and then quickly pushed it out of my mind.

One day the landlord, who had become our friend by this time, dropped in. Casually I asked him if he would consider selling the house. With great conviction, he said never. He and his wife had spent a whole year looking at a hundred houses at least before they finally found this one which they wanted. Being a nice man, he said that he would help us look for a house whenever we were ready to buy.

Four months later, he passed by again and said that he had been offered a very attractive job in another state but he would not accept it. Another month went by and he came again. He asked tentatively: "If I take the job offer, would you buy the house?" I said not at this time because harvest time in the Philippines, from where I would get the funds, was not due for another year.

One more month passed. He came again and said he had accepted the job, so I may buy his house. I said I did not have the money. But he said: "Can you sign a promissory note for the down payment? Then I can help you get the mortgage on the property." I signed the promissory note and he looked for a mortgage company.

On the date of the closing, I needed twenty five thousand dollars, which we did not have. Then Mario very casually said: "Oh, Mommy, I forgot to tell you that you have a letter from your caretaker in the Philippines." I opened the letter and there was a check in the equivalent of twenty five thousand dollars, my share from the crop of the previous year. How can I ever thank God for all these never-ending blessings?

The house on Military Road became "a house of God," as many of our friends used to call it. Everything happened in that house. Relatives from the Philippines came and stayed with us for months. Friends of my sons from their school in Manila came and stayed for years. A young pregnant girl from a prominent American family in New Jersey left her home, so she stayed in my room because there was no other room in the house.

A black couple, evicted from their home, came with their big dog and stayed for months. The medical oncology group from Georgetown held parties in our house. My son's singing group practiced and hung around.

Home Masses were offered in our house every month. My prayer group held its weekly meetings in our living room, and on and on. It was truly God's house because everyone was welcome to stay. The sense of peace and joy was palpable the moment you entered the front door.

It had a sad ending though. We lost it to the bank. The Marcos regime in the Philippines caused the collapse of many businesses, including ours. In 1983, I had to declare bankruptcy and the bank took over the property. It was painful to let go but the house belonged to God. He had loaned it to me and my children and the many people for whom it was a refuge or who shared happy days in it with us. For that, I am grateful. What they say is true: "God gives and God takes away. Blessed be the Lord." To this day, every time I pass by the house, I see it with a tinge of sadness, but the sadness is fleeting and momentary. Life goes on.

Of the house on Military Road, memories abound. It was there where I discovered the lump on my right breast which was cancer and from where my son Mario drove me to the hospital for cancer surgery.

It was there where the Hospice of Northern Virginia was planned. It was there also where the International Hospice Institute was born. Both these hospices were founded on March 19, the feast of Saint Joseph, my patron, namesake and dear friend.

There were other happy moments to remember. From this house, my daughter went on her first date with a young man who later became her husband. In this house, my second son Vince met his future wife. So did my son Cesar. In this house, God showered us with many, many blessings.

In the kitchen, we had a round table for four. It was not unusual for ten people to sit around it, enjoying a meal or snacks, with much laughter and happy conversation. Our table in the formal dining room was the scene of crab feasts. Our visitors from the Philippines, who came in big groups, enjoyed the famous Maryland crabs. We covered the table with newspapers, placed dozens of crabs on it and enjoyed the meal. It was so much fun.

One of my sons went through a motorcycle phase, which seemed inevitable at that time among high school boys. He had a motorcycle gang who wore black leather jackets and had weird hair. One day my son asked if I would cook a Filipino dinner for them. I asked how many they were going to be and he said twenty-four. I took it all very calmly.

On the day of the party, I used the best china and the best silver, and all the guests arrived. Twelve motorcycles, each carrying a boy and a girl in black leather jackets, zoomed down Military Road and parked in front of our house. The neighbors must have been horrified.

Before we started the meal, I invited everyone to pray and I did pray very intensely for all of them. It was a nice evening. After the dinner, all of them went to the kitchen and cleaned up; everything was shiny and orderly.

Then they had a little program in the living room. One by one, they took off a patch from their jackets and presented each to me in appreciation. The next day, they sent me a dozen red roses with a card which said: "To Mommy, with love."

Tears came to my eyes. Here I was, thinking that I was dealing with a bunch of ill-mannered, uncouth individuals just because they rode motorcycles, and wore black jackets. Deep within, they were decent and respectable individuals who happened to be part of a culture different from mine. I was grateful for the lesson.

6

Yes, it is cancer

It was 1972. My room in our home on Military Road was on street level in the front of the house and at eleven o'clock one night, my son Carlo drove back from a party. I heard him arguing loudly with some people and I had this scary feeling that something was wrong. Instinctively, I put my right hand on my right breast and I felt this lump. I was not looking for it and I had only made a woman's characteristic gesture of fear and there it was. I felt around it some more, trying to convince myself that I was mistaken and there was no lump at all.

I did not sleep that night. I did not want to confide my fears to the children because they would not know what to do and I would only upset them. I grappled with my fears all by myself and when morning came, I had made a decision. I was not going to do anything about the lump. I would let it stay there and let God decide what to do with it.

The reason for this attitude was the fact that when my husband had a metastasis of his melanoma seven years after radical surgery, some of our colleagues in the medical profession had started to think that if we had left that stain in his eyelids alone, he probably would still be alive. It is amazing how physicians can talk themselves into believing something totally unscientific when it suits their purpose and allays their fears.

A lady with a Ph.D. in my office had for days been talking about the miraculous properties of Vitamin E. In fact, she and her husband had been taking this miracle substance for months and she attributed their perfect health to its effect on the human body. I began asking her more about it without telling her why I was so interested, and she was only too happy to have one more convert to her way of thinking. I bought the capsules and started to take them religiously. I still did not tell anyone about the lump in my breast.

A whole week passed and I began to see my children in a new light. If I died, what would happen to them away from home in a strange land? And slowly, I began to feel guilty about my decision not to do anything about the lump. I was afraid, but I was also selfish, thinking only about my own feelings and completely ignoring the implications of my decision. I started to pray, asking God to tell me what to do. I finally decided to consult a doctor. Not my friends nor the colleagues I worked with; the doctor had to be a total stranger who could be completely objective. He must not know me and must not care how I felt or how frightened I was. Even in that state, I was practical enough to plan things efficiently. The doctor's office and his hospital privileges should be close to my home, just in case I needed to go to a hospital. And the doctor should be the best surgeon on the staff; he should be the head of surgery of the hospital I would choose.

I looked in the yellow pages of the telephone directory and I dialed the hospital that I had chosen. I asked for the head of surgery, but I was told he was out of the country attending a conference, but that a certain Doctor O'Donnell was taking his calls for him. Did I want to talk to him? I decided he probably was good enough in surgery to be acting head of the department so I said yes. I was hoping he would say he would see me in one week, because I was still too frightened to let a doctor examine my lump. But he came on the line right away, and he said: "Why don't you come right now?" I said I was scared he would find that I had cancer and I did not want to know. And then he said: "It is probably benign, but in the event it is malignant, we can always do something about it. There is only one way to find out and it is to do a biopsy. You can check into the hospital tonight and I can do the biopsy tomorrow, and you can then forget all about being afraid." It was Sunday.

He gave me his credentials over the phone. He was a graduate of Georgetown University school of medicine, he was a Catholic, and he had nine children. He talked about his post-graduate training, but at that point, I was convinced that he could be my surgeon. He was obviously a good man.

I then confided the whole thing to my son Mario. He turned pale, but he showed no panic. Instead he called Pat, a good friend of ours, and asked her to accompany me and him to the Doctors Hospital of Northern Virginia. And then I started to cry. I was washing the breakfast dishes and through the window, I saw Mario walking in our garden at the back, and his shoulders were bent and he was crying. I ran to my bathroom and cried and cried, because I could not bear his grief. The other two boys were more composed because they were totally helpless. They felt that the courage was there between Mario and myself, and things would work out.

On the way to the hospital, Pat, Mario and I passed by the Missionhurst Chapel and prayed. I was admitted that same night.

The hospital did all the tests and procedures necessary for surgery that night and I was probably given something to help me sleep, because the next thing I knew I was being wheeled into the operating room the following morning. And then I woke up with a huge bandage on the right side of my chest.

Dr. O'Donnell walked into my room early that afternoon and sat on the side of my bed. He was very kind and gentle. He said the lump was malignant and he had to do a radical mastectomy that meant the removal of the breast together with all the lymph nodes in the axilla, and all the muscles of the right chest. He said that we would know the final pathology report later on, but that he felt I had an 85% chance of completely recovering from my malignancy.

My stay in the hospital was a heartwarming experience because so many people came to visit or sent flowers and cards in a constant stream. My hospital room was not big enough to contain my visitors so the hospital allowed me to sit outside in the patio and meet with my guests. Someone who did not know what was going on could have easily concluded that I was conducting a seminar of some sort.

My post-operative recovery was uneventful, as doctors' charts are prone to say. I did not have too much pain and after five days I was discharged home. Volunteers from a post-mastectomy group came to see me in the hospital to show how natural breast prostheses had become, and how I could wear any kind of dress I wanted. They showed me how to do the exercises which would prevent my right arm from swelling. My children of course came to visit, but they all had to sit outside to make room for the visitors. All that show of affection and concern from friends and co-workers gave them much comfort in their own pain. It gave them joy to know that they were not alone.

I found out much later that three days after my surgery, Mario called a meeting of his siblings and said to them: "Mommy has cancer. We do not know for how long or how short is the time that she will be with us, so we should know what we are going to do if she dies." One by one he asked them: would they go back to the Philippines? Would they stay in the United States and continue with their studies? I do not know what each one said, but I remember Mario's plans. He had always wanted to become a Trappist monk and that is what he was going to do.

He went to Berryville and filed an application for admission. The monks loved him, but they said he was making a decision during a very emotional time because of his mother's illness and he should wait a year and then come back. The year passed and, in the process, Mario knew that the monastery was not where God wanted him. But he had tried.

I had a few positive nodes, so the doctors suggested adjuvant chemotherapy to prevent recurrence and metastasis. I thought about this very seriously and prayed about it. At that time, chemotherapy was still in an experimental stage. This meant that if I had chemotherapy, I might or might not have a recurrence. If I had chemotherapy, I would lose my hair, and I would feel the side effects of that treatment. I was sure I did not want to lose my hair, and I was sure that if I only had one year of life left, I would want it to be a normal one-year, doing all the things that I was doing.

I refused chemotherapy and my doctors respected my decision. Then they said, what about radiation therapy? There are no side effects, and it will be a course of treatment of only five weeks, Monday to Friday. Since I was a physician, my job at George Washington University Hospital allowed me an indefinite number of sick days. I was going to say no again, but my children intervened.

If I died without any treatment at all-no chemotherapy and no radiation-they said they would be grieving that if only I had done something, I could still be alive. This convinced me that I had a responsibility towards them and that I was not alone by myself when such big decisions were to be made. I agreed to have the five weeks of radiation treatment.

Those five weeks of radiation treatments allowed me to see cancer patients at close range as I sat in the waiting room of the hospital. I would chat with the patients and their families and I discovered the terrible anguish and suffering they were all going through. As a physician, I knew some of the patients awaiting treatment could be dead in a few weeks, but they were still saying: "When I get well, Doctor …" My heart ached and that was when I decided I would be an oncologist and help discover the cure for cancer. I applied for and soon obtained a fellowship in medical oncology-one of the first four fellows-at Georgetown University Hospital.

God had enabled me to see the purpose of my breast cancer. He was opening new doors for me by drawing me to oncology because in that specialty, I would discover the main purpose of my existence: hospice care.

7

The seed of hospice

Without my realizing it, by July 1976, I had been in the United States for seven years. All my children had joined me. Instead of the one-bedroom furnished apartment which was our first home in Washington, D.C., we now had a four-bedroom house which we rented at first and which, in God's providence, we bought. After breast surgery, I had no more symptoms of cancer. Life was good and my children had many friends, both Filipino and American, who came in and out of our house at all hours. But still I did not know how to drive a car. In the Philippines when I left, it was uncommon for a woman to drive. If she could afford a car, she could also afford to pay a driver. During all the time when I was working both at George Washington University Hospital and at HEW, I took the bus. Providentially the bus stop was right in front of our house, so it was like being driven to and from work in a chauffeured limousine. Moreover the bus ride gave me many moments of thought and prayer and was a very pleasant way to begin and end each day. When I moved to Georgetown University Hospital, my whole life changed. The bus stop in front of our house did not service the buses to Georgetown. I needed three transfers to go to work and to return home. My two youngest sons assumed the responsibility of driving me to work and then picking me up at the end of the day when they were through with their classes. For everyone concerned, it was a difficult time. Until now I can imagine the great embarrassment that the two boys endured each day when they had to excuse themselves from school activities or from their friends because they had "to pick up Mom". But we managed to endure the inconvenience.

One day a patient was assigned to me, a very glamorous lady with metastatic breast cancer. Her family was extremely devoted to her and I became friends with all her children. She had been in the realty business. In one of our casual conversations, I told her that my sons picked me up from work and that this must be difficult for them. She said: "Why don't you learn to drive? I started driving when I was 56 years old and I never realized what I had been missing during the time when I was dependent on others to bring me places." I was also 56 years old when she talked to me.

I gave the matter a great deal of thought. Then one day I looked at the ads in the yellow pages which offered driving lessons "for nervous beginners." I did not tell anyone but I called Sears Roebuck and took driving lessons. In a week's time, I was ready for practice driving in which any of my sons could help me. Before long we trooped to a used car dealer to buy a second-hand car for me. We chose a white car with a blue interior. The salesman said it belonged to a diplomat from Argentina who took good care of it. That made me feel good.

Why all these details about driving lessons and getting a car? Not even in my wildest dreams did I envision myself driving a car. But God knows every detail of our lives, what we need and what He makes possible. He keeps telling us: "Just love me and I will take care of everything for you." He also says: "My grace is all you need."

A fellowship in medical oncology in a prestigious institution like Georgetown University Hospital is serious business. My children were appalled when they learned that I had taken on a two-year fellowship almost 20 years after I graduated from medical school. "Mommy, how can you do it?" they said. In my heart, I knew that I cannot but God can.

The work in the cancer ward was very difficult. cancer patients who go to a research and training institution like Georgetown University medical center have been diagnosed and treated in smaller hospitals. Usually very sick, they came to us looking for a miracle. They believed that Georgetown would have the cure.

One such patient was a gentleman from Cuba. He was 55 years old, diagnosed with cancer of the pancreas. He had terrible pains, accompanied by continuous nausea and vomiting. I would admit him into the hospital, relieve his pain and other symptoms, then send him home.

Three days later, he would be back in the emergency room with more pain, more nausea and more vomiting. I would admit him again, relieve his symptoms and send him home. These back-and-forth admissions, which are characteristic in terminal illness, happened about five more times.

His wife came to me and said: "Doctor I beg you. Please keep him in the hospital. My boss warned me that if I am absent one more day, I will be fired from my job. I am the only breadwinner in my family." I kept the patient in the hospital until he died several days later.

Another patient was Jack who was 60 years old. He was a white-haired gentleman who was surrounded by an extremely loving family: his wife and four daughters. They accompanied him to the hospital, hovering and fussing over him.

During those consultations, his wife would intercept me outside the examination room to say: "Doctor, please do not tell him that he has cancer. He does not know and it is better for him not to know."

One day I was in the examination room with Jack while his family waited outside. He said: "Doctor, please tell me the way it is. I sort of know, but I want you to tell me." So I did. He took it very calmly and philosophically. He asked if it would help if he went to Sloan Kettering Memorial Cancer Center in New York. I said if it made him feel better, I would arrange all his records and help him to be admitted. I did that but he and his family decided to stay with Georgetown.

A few months later, Jack was an in-patient in the hospital, terminally ill with lung cancer. He was a very nice and accommodating gentleman even during those last days of his life. He was in severe pain. I asked my boss if I could give him a morphine injection to relieve some of his pain. Classically at that time, my boss said: "He might get addicted." I begged and begged until he allowed me to give Jack 25 mg. by subcutaneous injection. That was a drop in the bucket. Today terminally ill patients can be given hundreds, even thousands, of milligrams of morphine to ensure that they are free from pain.

There were many patients whom I cared for during those two years of my training in oncology, but I remember Jack and the Cuban gentleman with special clarity. Through them, God was telling me some important truths about His dying children.

The days flew fast at the medical oncology division in Georgetown as we became busier. More referrals came from physicians and hospitals. More very sick patients came. It was hard work. Even more, it was heartbreaking work.

Research from many parts of the United States and the world brought in new information on newer medications or newer combinations of medications to destroy cancer cells. We were trying them all. Patients who were terminally ill clung to the last straw, hoping against hope that they might be the one or two per cent cited by literature as responsive to the new treatment. But with the new experimental medications came more devastating side effects which subtracted more from the quality of the patient's remaining life.

I watched all these with an aching heart, aching not only for the patients and their families but also for the whole medical system. If it was obvious that cure of the disease was no longer possible, why do we have to continue treating the patient at such great cost, not only in terms of human suffering but in financial resources? Is there another way by which we can continue to be healers? In what other manner can we sustain that miracle of hope, which some writers use to explain why patients continue to cling tenaciously to medical treatments even when these are no longer effective? As these queries ran in my mind, I found a little pamphlet on hospice care. From it, I learned about Dr. Cicely Saunders who started the concept of hospice in England for patients who are no longer curable. While a nurse and a social worker in World War II, Dr. Saunders saw many dying servicemen screaming in pain. She felt that allowing people to die in such great pain was cruel and inhuman. After the war, she went to medical school, the better to focus her mind and efforts on the control of pain in the dying.

After graduation from medical school, Dr. Saunders became the medical director of St. Joseph's Hospice, a 110-bed facility in West London. The Irish Sisters of Charity founded St. Joseph's to provide care for terminally ill patients.

In the early 60s, one of Dr. Saunder's patients gave her a small grant for one window in a hospice which he believed she should establish. In 1967 that dream came true with the opening of St. Christopher's Hospice, a 55-bed facility in Sydenham, a suburb of London.

Soon St. Christopher's became the show place for the whole world to see that it is possible for terminally ill patients to die painlessly, peacefully and with great dignity. St. Christopher's became the Mecca for medical professionals, non-professionals, caregivers and volunteers who came from all over the world to learn how to care for the dying.

The pamphlet was obviously God-sent to me. It answered many painful doubts and questions in my mind. What is the practice of medicine all about? Is it only to cure patients of disease? Should we not also provide them with comfort and support when the disease is incurable and they slip toward death? Should we not be there to hold a patient's hand, just be there for him, when we know that there is nothing to offer in terms of cure? Why should we insist on trying to cure when cure is no longer possible?

I went to my boss and told him about this new concept of care called hospice. I said that I would like to go to St. Christopher's Hospice to learn about what they were doing for the terminally ill. Like a true scientist, he did not get too excited about the idea. I had to beg and beg before he allowed me to go.

8

Learning hospice at St. Christopher's

The pamphlet about hospice care that I read by chance did not go into great detail about St. Christopher's. Other than saying that the founder was Dr. Cicely Saunders and that it was in London, the pamphlet did not give any specific address. After I got the permission to go, I wrote Dr. Saunders and sent the letter to London, England. I asked her if I may come to see what she was doing. I was not really expecting a reply because of the vague address that I wrote. But she did reply and she said come.

I had never been to England. I had absolutely no idea about what I was getting into, but as usual God was watching out for me. Shortly before I left, I met an Episcopalian minister who was leaving for London that very day. He knew where St. Christopher's was. He offered to meet me at the airport and take me to the hospice, and he did.

When I got to St. Christopher's I had mixed feelings-excitement, hope and the yearning to learn but also nervousness about seeing so many dying persons. As I had seen in pictures in the pamphlet, there was the insignia on the building showing St. Christopher carrying the Child Jesus on his shoulder. Everything was new to me: the lobby, the uniforms, the way people spoke, the way nurses were called Sisters and the physicians were called Registrars.

At that time, the hospice was a facility of 55 beds and admitted only terminally ill patients, both men and women. Patients do not occupy private rooms but are in bays with six to eight beds each. The reason is: a dying patient gets very frightened when he wakes up alone in the night. With other patients in the room, he will be less afraid.

During the days and weeks that patients spend together in the same bay, a supportive sense of camaraderie and of community develops. No one ever feels alone.

The other reason is that some patients do not have family members or friends visiting them. In a shared bay, the visitors of other patients become the visitors of the others. Relatives of one patient eventually become friends with the other patients and an atmosphere of gaiety prevails especially if small children are around.

The third reason is group prayer. In the morning, before the physicians and nurses make their rounds, they first stand at the threshold of the bays. They read a passage from Holy Scripture and then they say prayers together. The practice impressed me deeply because it connects the patient and the professional staff with God as they go about their day.

Since the problems that beset most dying patients are pain, loneliness and loss of control over circumstances, the hospice concentrates on relieving these problems. The primary diagnosis is unimportant. What matters are the symptoms which the patient suffers.

If it is pain, efforts are directed to relieve it. If it is loss of appetite or nausea or vomiting or constipation, every medication is employed to make him feel better. Vital signs are seldom taken and IV fluids are not given. The guiding principle is the patient's comfort. Anything that will cause him distress is avoided.

Dr. Saunders believes that since pain no longer is needed to help in the diagnosis and treatment of disease in a dying patient, it should be relieved unless the patient chooses to suffer from it for its redemptive value when it is united to the suffering of Christ. Dr. Saunders-together with cancer specialists, Dr. Robert Twycross and Dr. Richard Lamerton-have devoted a great deal of their time and effort to the control of pain. They have proven that pain can be eliminated provided that the right analgesics are given in adequate dosage and at regular intervals around the clock. The pain has to be so controlled that the patient has no memory of it.

Any visitor to St. Christopher's Hospice-or to any one of today's well-managed hospices-will not fail to be impressed at how free from pain the dying patients are in these facilities. Many of them are able to sit up in bed or visit with their families.

Some women knit or crochet little items when they are able and these are later on given to their families to remind them of the tranquility which characterized the last moments of life.

The men are encouraged to work on simple projects such as basket-weaving and wood carving. If they are in pain, these activities would be impossible and the quality of life would be unbearable, not only for the patients but for their families.

When I went there, St. Christopher's Hospice had three floors. Dr. Saunder's apartment was on the third floor and she kindly allowed me to stay there throughout my visit. Patients occupied the second floor and part of the third floor. Meals were served in the dining room on the first floor.

Loneliness is a terrible feeling, much more so when a person is dying. At St. Christopher's, visiting hours are unrestricted except for one day a week in order to give both patient and family a respite from the strain of visiting. Children can come to spend the day. Even pets can be brought to visit. Once a week, a bar is opened so that the patients, if they wish, can be wheeled to the lounge and socialize with guests, staff and one another.

Mealtimes were a tremendous experience for me since I came from an acute tertiary care hospital. Before each meal, the staff prepares the patients by combing their hair and helping them into their best and prettiest robes. Propped up in bed, they are served the meal on a tray with fresh and crisp linen napkins, silverware and a flower in a vase.

Soup comes first. The patient is allowed to take all the time to enjoy it. No one is rushed and the staff is not hurrying. After the soup, the plates are changed for the main course and complete sidings. While portions are kept small, they are served very attractively in order to whet the appetite. After the main course comes the dessert. Wine is served before, during or after the meal as the patient wishes.

Admission to St. Christopher's is by referral from hospitals after the attending physician makes a prognosis of terminal illness. Upon admission, the patient is wheeled directly into his assigned bay so that he can receive immediate attention. The paper work is accomplished later on by family members.

The patient is allowed to use his own clothes and to keep some of his favorite possessions with him. From then on, he is involved in the decision-making about every aspect of his care, including the medications that are offered to make him comfortable. He is encouraged to do things for himself if he is able, such as choosing from the menu, washing his face or combing his hair. He may do passive exercises with the physical therapist. An occupational therapist provides games and things to do to fight feelings of boredom, helplessness and loneliness.

Every patient is given the option to refuse anything. No one is ever awakened so that the temperature can be taken. The patient is the most important member of the hospice team and anything that distresses him is avoided. His comfort determines the activities he is asked to do.

At St. Christopher's, there is a screaming room which they probably originated. Located away from everything, it is the place where family members can scream without worrying about being heard. In this room, cries of grief, anger and frustration are vented in any degree.

The chapel is an important part of St. Christopher's. The doors open wide to let in the patients' beds. With family members, visitors and the staff, the patients attend the religious services. I found the chapel to be a haven of peace and tranquility.

Before I arrived at St. Christopher's, I was apprehensive. A place where 55 patients are dying must be a very morbid place, I thought. I discovered that while it was true that they were dying, they were dying without pain, in peace and with dignity. At this point, I said to myself: We must have this kind of hospice in the United States. We can do all the things that they are doing here. We have the expertise for pain and symptom control. We have the caring attitude. And we have the financial resources. This was the moment when the idea of a hospice program at Georgetown University Hospital entered my mind.

9

"Do whatever you need to do"

What I saw and learned at St. Christopher's Hospice seemed so right for terminally ill patients for whom cure of disease was no longer possible. However, there were many, many questions that needed answers before anything could even be planned.

First of all, there was the question of funds. Hospice was a strange word in the American vocabulary at that time. When I mentioned the word, an inevitable blank look came to the face of the person to whom I was talking. Moreover, even familiar projects on well-understood concepts required reams of paper work, application forms, interviews, committee meetings and so on before they could be funded. Dealing with a prestigious research institution like Georgetown University Medical Center made this process even more daunting, because there were many other worthwhile projects that could be funded.

When I am helpless, I have learned to turn to God's help. I went to the hospital chapel and discussed this problem with Him who had put the idea into my head in the first place. Then I proceeded to the office of Rev. Timothy Healy, S.J., the president of Georgetown University. I simply told him: "Father, we need a hospice in Georgetown." He of course looked at me with a half-smile of incredulity and asked: "Jo, what is a hospice?" I explained the concept to him and what I learned at St. Christopher's Hospice and how I felt that they could be applicable in the United States.

After my explanation, Father Healy got up and said the famous words: "Jo, if hospice is the humane care of the dying, that is the mission of a Catholic hospital. Georgetown must not only have a hospice program, it must have a leadership role in the hospice movement in the country. Do whatever you need to do. I will support you." God had provided the answer.

Still I needed the money to start anything. I knew that had I approached the hospital administrator, he would ask me to write a proposal, create a committee to evaluate it, and it would take at least a year before any action would be taken.

Meantime, patients were dying in our oncology ward, many of them in great pain. They could not wait that long. There had to be a faster, more efficient way to get hospice going for them.

I went to the medical records division of the hospital and reviewed the charts of as many patients as I could. I discovered that 65% of our cancer patients were covered by Blue Cross/Blue Shield medical insurance. Since many of them had died, it was easy to determine how much Blue Cross/Blue Shield had spent on each patient and, specifically, how much was spent during the last six months of their lives. It was also easy to calculate how much insurance companies pay for a vacant bed in the hospital to cover the expensive equipment, as well as faculty, staff and administrative expenses.

Armed with this information, I went to the head office of Blue Cross/Blue Shield and talked to the then acting president of the company. I explained what I had found out: how his firm was spending $600 a day for a vacant bed in the hospital as well as so many thousands of dollars on the last stages of a cancer patient's hospitalization when he no longer needed all the expensive diagnostic procedures and interventions. I explained to him the hospice concept of care for the terminally ill and how much money it would save Blue Cross/Blue Shield if we had a hospice program in Georgetown.

I asked him to assign two of his vice presidents to work with me on a Georgetown University Blue Cross/Blue Shield pilot project on hospice care. The project would determine if the hospice concept of care as practiced in England was suitable to American culture and mores and what impact the hospice concept of care would have on American patients and their families. The project would also serve to document the actual cost of hospice care and how it compares with conventional hospital care.

Before the project was finally approved for submission to both the boards of directors of Blue Cross/Blue Shield and of Georgetown University, I was asked one crucial question. What guarantee can Blue Cross/Blue Shield have that Georgetown University Hospital will not dump all its unwanted patients on the project?

My answer was quick: "We will limit admission to the pilot project only to patients who have a prognosis of life expectancy of six months or less." (Years later, the data from our pilot project was used by the US Congress to pass an amendment in the Social Security Act, requiring hospice care reimbursement by Medicare and Medicaid. It became a joke among hospice circles that I should have said "a prognosis of at least a year or two.")

At that time, hospice care in the US. was patterned after St. Christopher's Hospice which is in-patient care in a facility. We therefore needed at least six beds to make our pilot project a reality.

I approached the Georgetown University Hospital administrator and asked if I might have six beds somewhere in the hospital for our project. Of course, he asked what hospice is and what it entails. I explained to him that family members and children and even pets would be allowed to visit and stay with the dying relative. He was aghast, to put it mildly, and kindly told me that it was impossible to have even children set foot inside the hospital, much less cats and dogs.

He was very kind though. He pointed out that Georgetown University Hospital was affiliated with a nursing home, located just a few blocks away. The patients in this nursing home were in the care of Georgetown University physicians. The place might be considered to house our hospice project.

I proceeded to this nursing home, then called Washington Home for Incurables, a legacy of several wealthy women. I started talking to the administrator. He was a deeply religious man, a minister in his church. He readily understood the concept of hospice care based on humane compassion for patients who were nearing the end of life.

I prepared a give-and-take proposal. The nursing home provides our project with a separate unit with its own entrance, six beds, room and board, housekeeping and maintenance. In turn, the project pays the nursing home a fixed amount for these facilities as well as nursing care, medications and other direct patient needs. We came to an agreement. Thus, our project became known as the Georgetown University/Blue Cross/Blue Shield/Washington Home Pilot Project on Hospice Care. We inaugurated it in May 1978 with TV cameras and many dignitaries present.

We calculated the cost per day based on these following items: cost for room and board and maintenance; cost of beautifying the hospice unit with colorful wallpaper, new bedspreads, TV sets, plants and so forth, divided among six patients per day per year; cost of nursing care at one nurse per three patients per shift; cost of medication; and cost for administrative staff. The cost per day amounted to half the cost if the patient had been confined at Georgetown University Hospital.

In 1980 when I left Georgetown to be the first executive director of the National Hospice Organization, the pilot project was taken over by George Washington University Hospital. In 1996, it was returned to Georgetown University Hospital. Meanwhile, the Washington Home developed its own hospice program.

While developing the pilot project on hospice care with Blue Cross/Blue Shield, I got a phone call from the secretary general of the Knights of Malta. He asked me to give a talk on the hospice concept of care at their annual meeting. It would be a white tie dinner in one of the exclusive clubs in Washington.

When I said I would, he told me that someone would pick me up at a certain time and to please remember that the affair was very formal: it was white tie and not black tie.

These details were understandable because the Knights of Malta represent the elite in business, industry, the arts and the sciences from all over the United States. The president of the Knights of Malta at that time was an international contractor with businesses in many parts of the globe. He was at dinner in South America at the home of a business associate, and he was served wine which had such an extraordinary quality that he asked where it came from. His host said there were only four cases available in the world, but he could have them if he wanted them. It was this wine that was served at the annual meeting dinner of the Knights of Malta where I was invited to give the talk on hospice care.

Given this type of background of the event, I was naturally terrified. I said to myself that while I had been giving extemporaneous talks on hospice care on many other occasions, I had to really write a good paper for this particular audience. I had to be well prepared.

I tried to write a talk. I prayed hard and I tried and tried to write something, but I always ended up with a blank sheet of paper. The event was coming closer and I still did not have anything prepared by way of a talk.

I finally got the message which God had been trying to tell me. I cannot give a talk by myself, but with His help I can, so all I need to do is ask Him and then trust Him to speak through me, regardless of whom the audience will be. I gave up trying to write a talk and decided to do just that: pray and let God speak through me.

The night of the gala event came and as previously arranged, someone in white tie came to pick me up. What I did not know was that the Knights of Malta had their annual meeting without any ladies. Their wives were at a formal dinner in the president of the Knights' home at the same time. With this information, I walked with my escort into a room full of distinguished-looking gentlemen in white ties, with Bishops and Archbishops and Cardinals in their full regalia. I was the only lady present.

At dinner, I was seated between the president of the Knights and the cardinal from the archdiocese of Washington, D.C.. I still had no notes in hand. The dinner was superb; the atmosphere was very formal and elegant. After dessert, I was introduced as the speaker for the evening. I prayed and I was very peaceful. I gave the talk on the hospice concept of care without any notes but from my heart. The audience was very quiet and everyone listened in rapt attention. When I finished the talk, I sat down and the entire assembly rose to its feet and gave me a standing ovation.

God had succeeded in giving me the message that from henceforth, I must know that whenever I give a talk on hospice care, it would be God speaking through me. He knows what the audience needs to hear and He would put the words in my mouth. I have kept that in mind through the years, and whenever I give a talk on hospice care, it is always without a written text, regardless of how big or small my audience is. I always pray hard, and God has never failed to hear my prayer.

While in Georgetown, I met a young man after one of the lectures on the hospice concept of humane care for the terminally ill that I gave to second year medical students. He stood out in the crowd-tall, handsome, brilliant, with the kind of bearing which the name Adonis conjures. He was from a well-to-do family in New Jersey. He finished pre-medicine, *summa cum laude,* at Princeton and had been accepted by all the top medical schools in the US to which he applied. He chose Georgetown University, but did not enroll after all. He felt inadequate to start medical school. Instead he went to Sorbonne and took a year of philosophy. Still he did not feel ready for medical school. So he went to Oxford and studied literature for a year. Then he thought he was finally ready and enrolled in Georgetown to start becoming a doctor. After my lecture on hospice, he came to me with tears in his eyes. He said: "Doctor, you have just saved my life." He said that he began medical school with great ideals and aspirations of serving mankind as the best physician he could be. Less than two years into medical school, he thought, "they are trying to make a technician out of me." He became so disillusioned and so depressed that he wanted to die.

When he heard my lecture, he said he realized that, yes, it was possible to be a technician and still care about people and serve mankind. He kept up with me and we became good friends. One day he gave me a present to remember him by: a beautiful set of a chalice and paten. He knew that the Mass was celebrated in my home for family and friends. I am happy to say that he finished medical school, became a pediatrician and married a beautiful lady physician.

I was on my third year of training in medical oncology at Georgetown University Hospital when, in the elevator one morning, someone said to me: "Did you see your picture in the papers today?" Much later in the day, I did see it-a huge picture of me in my white lab coat with the caption: "This physician's patients all died." There is probably no worse advertisement for any physician but the very morbid caption called people's attention, and they read on.

The accompanying article explained hospice care and what it can do for patients for whom cure of disease is no longer possible. When this moment comes in the patient's life, the focus of management should shift from *curing* to *caring*. The efforts of the hospice team focus on maximizing the quality of the patient's remaining life by making him as free from pain and other symptoms as possible, and providing him and the members of his family with the support that they all need during this very stressful time. Thus, from unexpected sources, hospice care was being brought to the attention of the public. It would take a lot of time, but hospice was beginning to grow into people's awareness and understanding. Divine Providence was at work.

10

The Hospice of Northern Virginia

The Georgetown University/Blue Cross/Blue Shield pilot project on hospice care had been in existence for six months when, one cold blustery December night, two dear friends of mine knocked on our door on Military Road. They were Dorothy Garrett and Pat Pastore. Given the time and the bad weather, I knew they had come for something serious.

As soon as they had taken off their coats and sat down, they almost simultaneously said: "You have the Georgetown hospice project, but not everyone can go to Georgetown. How do you propose to take care of the rest of the terminally ill patients in Northern Virginia?" I said, very simply, "Let us start a hospice of Northern Virginia."

Dorothy Garrett is an excellent administrator and community leader and Pat Pastore is probably one of the most caring nurses in the country. Dorothy took out her notebook and her calculator, and we started talking and planning a community-based hospice home care program. We had no money, but that did not deter us. We talked for a long time, into the wee hours of the night. By the time we were through, we had everything all lined up, including the board of directors.

The next step was to call the potential board members. I wrote notes inviting them to come to a meeting in my home. They did not know what hospice was, nor what the meeting was all about, but these were friends from church and so they came.

Dorothy, Pat and I explained what the hospice concept is and what we were planning to do. The chief executive of Arlington County at the time, Joseph Wholey, was also a dear friend, so we involved him from the very beginning. This was very useful because he taught us the intricacies of the political system and how to deal with it. We still had no money, but I remember how we all sat on the floor of my house and prayed and asked God to guide us.

There was an advantage in the fact that I was working with Georgetown University Hospital and that I was the medical director of the Georgetown pilot project on hospice care. In this capacity, it was possible for me to make house calls and talk about the hospice concept of care to the community from an academic standpoint. This was important because hospice care was a relatively unknown subject at the time.

Since we had no funds to hire staff, we approached the Visiting Nurses Association and entered into a contract with them. We divided Northern Virginia into four regions, and then we assigned one VNA nurse to each region. We chose the nurses who had the capability and the temperament to take care of dying patients. We thus had a medical director and four nurses in the staff of the Hospice of Northern Virginia. We needed a social worker and a secretary, and we needed an office. Rev. Hoffman of The Church of the Covenant, a few blocks away from my house offered us office space, rent free, and very soon we had a volunteer social worker and a secretary.

Word about the care that was being provided to terminally ill patients in their homes by Hospice of Northern Virginia soon began to spread. The newspapers picked it up and wrote feature articles which caught the attention of the public. I was giving talks on the concepts of hospice care to community gatherings, civic organizations, medical societies, hospitals, parish meetings, and to anyone who would listen. Referrals started to come in, first a few and then more and more, until we had a good home care program going. Grateful families started to send donations and the time came when we needed an administrator who could attend to the management of the program, secure state licensures, solicit funds and so on.

The board of directors decided that we needed an administrator with a good experience in health care, had at least a master's degree in the health sciences and expertise in dealing with legislatures, was articulate and could write well. In other words, we needed someone whom we definitely could not afford given the state of our negative finances. But we had faith and so we advertised for such a person. And God sent the right individual except that what we could afford in terms of salary was only one-third of what she needed. Impossible situation? By this time, God had given us free office space, a volunteer staff, a medical director paid by Georgetown University Hospital (myself) and four nurses who were on a subcontract with VNA. If we had an administrator to pull everything together, Hospice of Northern Virginia would no longer be a dream but a reality.

We told our potential administrator that we could afford only one-third of what she was asking, but that we could not ask her to lower her salary request.

She said her husband had just moved into the area on a new job, and she could probably work for only one third of her time instead of full time. God had answered our prayers once again and Hospice of Northern Virginia was in business.

The first thing that had to be done was to identify all the requirements that the state of Virginia had imposed on hospices at the time. It was 1978, hospice was very new in the country, and both federal and state governments were gingerly finding their way through existing health care regulations that might be adapted or modified to suit the hospice model. Things like certificates of need (CON) as a means of controlling the number of hospice programs in a given area had to be defined, ways and means of requiring standards for licensure, methods and procedures for reimbursement of hospice services by the federal, state, and private insurers had to be drafted, and a myriad of other details were required at that period in the history of the hospice movement in America. Dorothy Moga, our administrator at the Hospice of Northern Virginia, plunged into all this paper work with great efficiency and tremendous knowledge and ability. She made numerous trips to Richmond, the capital of the state of Virginia, attended hearings and gave testimonies. I also had my share of these proceedings because the state needed to be sure.

Before too long, everything fell into place. Hospice of Northern Virginia having hurdled all the primary obstacles, was now a licensed agency, and could provide hospice home care the way it was intended.

I continued to be medical director of the community-based Hospice of Northern Virginia because the home care program had evolved into a facet of the pilot project on hospice care of Georgetown University Hospital. As part of the approach to introducing the concept of hospice care to physicians, I had secured permission from the chief of medical oncology at Georgetown to use fellows in medical oncology to make house calls on terminally ill patients in their homes. This was a good part of the program because the patients received expert medical attention, the young physicians were learning about hospice care and at the same time earning some extra spending money, and I had more time to attend to the inevitable mountain of paper work involved in the development of a new health care delivery system.

One humorous incident has to be told at this point because it is part of the history of Hospice of Northern Virginia. During this time, I had been driving only for two years. Hospice home care of course means visiting patients in their homes. In the early days of the program, I had to make house calls on three patients.

With a great deal of trepidation, and with maps, which did not quite make sense to me, given my relative inexperience in driving around, I ventured to make my house calls. I drove and drove and drove around northern Virginia, and two hours later, I had not located a single patient. Exhausted and frustrated, I dragged myself to the hospice office to report on my fiasco.

We had one volunteer at that time, Cynthia Todd, who was the general factotum of the organization. An emergency meeting of the staff was called, and a unanimous decision was made that henceforth one of the major functions of a hospice volunteer was to drive Jo Magno around to visit patients. The sad alternative was for Jo to continue driving around northern Virginia and not succeed in finding a single patient and we would have to close the organization.

This decision was inspired. Much later, many volunteers would report that their visits to patients in their homes with Jo were the highlights of their work in hospice. I brought the volunteer in with me the first time I saw a patient. I introduced her saying: "This is Mary. She is a volunteer with Hospice of Northern Virginia and we have asked her to be a volunteer to help you in any way you would like her to help."

Then I asked the patient or the spouse to give me a history of the present illness in a friendly, casual conversation and not at all like the history-taking in a hospital room or a doctor's office. Usually it started off this way: We were on a vacation in Florida four months ago. We had just finished dinner at a fancy restaurant and he complained of abdominal discomfort. We all said it was because he probably ate too much, and it would go away after he rested. But the pain persisted so we decided to go to the doctor the next day. The doctor suspected something so he asked for all kinds of tests. A diagnosis of cancer of the colon was made. He had surgery three months ago, but he continued not to feel well. The cancer had gone to the liver.

We talked about their children, their grandchildren and other family stories. By the time the visit was over, the volunteer already had a clear picture of what she was going to deal with. Since she was part of the initial conversation, she had become part of the inner circle so that the next time she visited, she was not a stranger and she did not have to ask any questions about the history of the disease.

Volunteers are the heart of hospice care. As I mentioned earlier, Cynthia Todd was the very first volunteer of Hospice of Northern Virginia. She was an excellent driver and she was single, so she had full control of her time. She drove me to see patients, and to speaking engagements when these were accessible by car. In her spare time, she continued to be secretary and general factotum of Hospice of Northern Virginia.

Ruth Joyner, a dear friend, was also one of the hospice's first volunteers. Ruth told me much later that I had asked for people to be volunteers for the hospice program and I had given a phone number to call. She called me right away, but I was not home, so she left a number and a message for me to return her call. I never did, so nothing happened.

Several months later, I gave a talk on hospice in her church and there she approached me and said she would like to be a volunteer with Hospice of Northern Virginia. So began our friendship which lasted for almost 20 years, until her death from cancer.

Ruth was the quiet type of person who did not stand out in a crowd. She talked with a hoarse voice, but she had a smile which brightened her whole face. She was very well read, and she could talk about anything under the sun. Her husband was a retired government executive when I first met Ruth. When he developed Alzheimer's disease, she had to put him in a nursing home three hours away by car from her own home. But rain or shine, snow and ice, Ruth got into her car and drove once a week to visit him. He did not recognize her, but Ruth went anyway.

Ruth had an elderly mother and she took her to live with her. She looked after her and her husband before his condition necessitated his stay in a nursing home. Ruth had a parrot, a gray and red bird which whistled and talked all the time. Because she had worked overseas in one of the government's CIA programs in Europe, she had many friends whom she visited at regular intervals. So her life revolved around her old mother, her ailing husband, her parrot, her volunteer work with hospice, her many friends and "adopted" children, many of whom stayed in her house for months and months. She was the soul of generosity.

One day, one of my friends from my parish called me to ask if I might provide room and board for a young girl from Colombia who was then taking up nursing at Marymount College. Unfortunately, I had a full house at the time but I said I would call my friends to see if anyone could help. I called Ruth and of course she said yes. She had a room and the girl could come right away. This was the beginning of Ruth's connection with the top echelon of Colombia's society. It turned out that the young girl's father was a justice of the Supreme Court in his country. He became the ambassador to Spain and then eventually the president. Ruth went to Spain and to Colombia and once again, she had formed another family. The girl from Colombia fell in love and got married. Her brother met Ruth and he ended up staying with Ruth also. This story was repeated over and over again with other personalities and gave Ruth many families to look after. She never failed anyone, her door was open all the time and she took in anyone who needed her help.

One of Ruth's obsessions was the care of the elderly and the terminally ill. In her mind, she envisioned a home care program for the elderly in their homes by volunteers, organized by her Episcopal church in order to alleviate their loneliness and sense of being abandoned. I had gone to live in Michigan and she called me one day and asked if I could fly to McLean, Virginia, so I could give a talk on the subject to her congregation. She was one of the elders. She added: "Nobody seems to take my ideas seriously, but if you are the one to say them, they might believe you." I did come to the church, gave a talk and discussed it with the rector. It was a good idea but nothing happened.

One day, at 10:00 in the morning, Ruth called me in Michigan and said out of the blue: "Jo, pray hard for me. I have advanced cancer and the doctors say I am going to die." I took the first flight to Washington, D.C., to visit her and find out what the situation was.

Ruth's husband had died two years earlier and her mother died six months after his death. Ruth was really all alone in the world in terms of family. She was getting chemotherapy for her cancer. As usual, she looked peaceful and she still had the wide smile that brightened her whole face.

I accompanied her to her treatment, and while the medicines were dripping into her vein, she held my hand and said: "I am leaving everything I own to you." And I said: "Why would you do that?" And she said: "Because you are my friend and you are doing important work and I want to help you continue doing hospice."

Ruth's death came faster than I expected. I had been in South Carolina giving a talk when I received a call from one of her friends telling me that she was sinking fast. I flew back to be with her, and I took care of her for about three days. And then I called Hospice of Northern Virginia. That call was the best one that I made, because hospice came right away. First, a well-dressed lady came bringing flowers. She introduced herself as the social worker from hospice. She had come to do the admission process and to assure me that they would take care of Ruth. "You can just be her friend because we will do everything else for her," she said.

Then the hospice nurse came. In the course of my many years' experience in hospice work, I never really felt until then the tremendous relief that comes to a family as soon as the hospice team walks into the door and takes over. It was almost as if a heavy physical burden was taken off from one's shoulders.

I used to say in talks to hospice staff: "We must know what we are doing. The patient and family are going through the most stressful time in their lives. There is chaos. There is fear. There is grief. There is anger. There is guilt. If we do not know what we are doing, and we are falling all over one another, we will only add to this chaos. But if we are competent, we can walk into the patient's room and into the innermost chambers of the heart. We can say with confidence: 'Do not worry. We will take care of everything for you.' And that is what they need to hear."

Many volunteers who had gone on home visits with me sometimes said: "It is amazing how we would walk into this home and find everything in chaos. One hour later, after the visit is over, there is calm and a sense of peace, and everything is really all right." I experienced this with Ruth when hospice came in to take care of her.

Ruth was with hospice only for two short days. One night, she wanted to get dressed to visit with a guest who was coming to the house. She was incoherent and I felt that the end was near. We put her to bed and watched her through the night. She had no pain and early in the morning, she quietly passed away. Another friend, Jean Bergaust, and I took care of the funeral arrangements. They were simple and dignified, befitting this wonderful lady who had lived for others all of her life.

Did she leave me everything she owned? In her mind, she did and for that I am grateful. But the lawyers said that was not written in her will so it did not count. And we left it at that.

Two years after that cold December night when Dorothy Garrett, Pat Pastore and I dreamed of Hospice of Northern Virginia and actually got it started, the hospice program was well established and functioning. Physicians were referring their terminally ill patients for hospice care, reimbursement was available, we had paid staff and things were good. Between the Georgetown Hospice Project and Hospice of Northern Virginia, I found myself pulled in all directions. In other words, I was tired.

A month earlier, I received a letter in the mail. It was from a lady physician who had just finished her training as an oncologist at the National Institute of Health (NIH). She was looking for a part-time job as medical director of Hospice of Northern Virginia: was one available? I tossed the letter aside because we did not have the funds nor the patients to require two hospice medical directors.

One morning, after a terribly busy day, I thought of this lady applicant who might be available to help part-time. I said if I can only find her letter of application which I had thrown away, just because it was so impossible to even consider it. And then I opened my desk drawer and there was her letter. I called her up and she came that afternoon for an interview.

This story is not about her eligibility for the position she was seeking. There was no question that her training as an oncologist more than qualified her for the job. What was amazing was the miracle of Beth's life and why she was a doctor. The remarkable thing about it was that she was so totally unaware of what God had been doing in her life to prepare her for this moment when she would be medical director of HNV.

Beth told me that she was one of two siblings. She had a younger brother. Their father was an executive of Westinghouse, they lived in Boston, the mother was a housewife, and they had a rather comfortable life. When Beth was in second year high school, her father became increasingly reflective and quiet. One day, he told his wife: "I have been hearing this call from God to be a minister, and I have tried to shake it off, but it wouldn't go away. I feel I have to obey and do what He wants me to do. I want to enter the seminary." The wife said: "Why don't you go? I can find a job, and the two children can wait on tables to help them through high school and college and we will be all right."

He resigned from his executive job *and* entered the seminary. Meanwhile, Beth and her brother finished high school and Beth graduated from college. She had wanted to be a physician all her life, but now the only chance for her to do that was to get a scholarship from somewhere. She sent applications to many schools of medicine always with a request for financial assistance. All of them turned her down. One day, she received a letter from Tufts University accepting her into their school of medicine. Beth went for the interview knowing that they had no money to finance her medical education. She did ask anyway if there was a chance that they might have a scholarship for which she could apply. They said no. All the scholarships had been given away. Beth went home thinking that it was a foolish dream to imagine that she could become a doctor.

Several days later, Beth got a phone call from Tufts University. Can she come for a second interview? The reason: the scholarship office had found an old document, dusty with age, of a grant which had been given to Tufts years earlier to support a student through medical school. It was never given to anyone, because the grant stipulated that "the recipient must be the daughter of a church minister." For years and years, no applicant had ever been close to this stipulation of the grant until Beth came along. God from all eternity had foreseen Beth's father's unselfishness and his daughter's desire to become a physician. And He granted it all. How can we not marvel at all these miracles that constantly happen around us in the most unexpected moments?

Beth became part-time medical director of HNV and she did a wonderful job. When I left HNV to become the first executive director of the National Hospice Organization, Beth became the medical director of Hospice of Northern Virginia. She has since become a successful full-time medical oncologist, but occasionally acts as consultant to HNV.

Early in the history of HNV, I was given an award by the Mortar Club of America, an organization of college women. The organizer of the awards banquet called me to say that a lady would pick me up. Her name was Peggy, and she was the cleaning lady at Missionhurst Chapel, which was close to my home.

The event came and I was dressed and waiting for Peggy, the cleaning lady, to pick me up. I was expecting to see an old car drive up to my house. Instead there was this big, sleek, pale-blue Oldsmobile, and a well-dressed lady coming out of the driver's seat. "I am Peggy," she said. I asked: "Are you the cleaning lady at Missionhurst?" I wanted to be sure I had the correct information. She smiled and said: "I do that, too." Peggy was the wife of Admiral Paul Hartman, and as the deeply religious Catholic woman that she is, she volunteered to clean the Missionhurst chapel every day.

Peggy and I became close friends. As a volunteer for HNV, her favorite assignment was to drive me to speaking engagements in Philadelphia, Maryland or Virginia. During those long drives, we talked about many things. One day she said to me: "Jo, please do not expect me to do patient care. I do not have the stomach for it." I said sure. So Peggy stayed on being a driver, a receptionist, a fund-raiser, and community leader.

Several years later, after I had moved on into the International Hospice Institute, she and I met and she said: "Guess what? I am taking care of the dying patients with their sores and their stench. I hold them in my arms, and I love every minute of it." God's miracles never cease.

11
"How long, Doctor?"

Eugene was 65 when he retired from his job as an engineer with the federal government. He was a brilliant man. He had been looking forward to retirement so he could finally indulge his hobbies of photography and classical music. He saved what he called "fun money" and he planned to spend all of it and really enjoy life after the many grueling years of hard work as a government employee. Then tragedy struck. He was diagnosed with advanced cancer of the prostate with metastasis to the bones. He was in great pain.

I was called by one of my colleagues in northern Virginia to see Eugene and help him through this last part of his life. He was at home, after having been discharged from one of the area hospitals where all the procedures and tests had been made and the diagnosis of terminal illness was made. He was referred for hospice care. It was ten o'clock in the morning when I made my first visit to Eugene in his home, a bungalow in one of the suburbs of metropolitan Washington. He was pale with a look of apprehension, almost fear, in his eyes. He was clearly depressed.

I introduced myself as the medical director of Hospice of Northern Virginia. I said I had been asked by his attending physician to see what he and I could do together to make him as comfortable as possible. We chatted for a while, and he began to relax and even smile every now and then. I asked him what it was that made him most uncomfortable and he said it was the pain in his bones.

Then his engineer's mind started to take over: "Why am I in pain, Doctor?" I explained to him the anatomy, the pathology, the physiology of why he was in pain. I went into what I intended to do to relieve his pain, making sure that he understood the pharmacology and the rationale for the medication that I was giving him. With all this information, he was satisfied. And he began to trust me.

Several days later, I made a second house call. This time Gene looked actually happy to see me. He was comfortable and his pain had gone away. But he had another question: "Why am I constipated, Doctor?" He then explained to me his own engineer's version of why he was constipated. He saw the gastro-intestinal tract as a system of pipes through which substance should flow freely and smoothly at regular intervals. If for some reason, there is an obstruction somewhere, or if the pipes are not in their proper places, then constipation occurs. As in the case of pain, I then explained the anatomy, the physiology and the pathology of why constipation occurs, and what must be done to remedy the prevailing problem, including the medicines that had to be taken. He was contented with this explanation and he found it easy to cooperate with everything I asked him to do.

Many more such visits happened during which we tackled his problems thoroughly, one by one. I teased him, saying that he was making a very good doctor out of me. Every time I visited him, I felt like I was taking my board examinations all over again since I had to really know the answers to his many questions.

One day I came to see Eugene again. As I entered his house, he said: "Doctor, this time I have a real problem." In my heart I said, what now? I asked him what the problem was, and he said: "I have thought and thought of something I can complain to you about and I cannot think of anything. How long will this dying business take me? It is so boring to be dying."

He had just asked the deepest philosophical question about dying. How long? I told him that I had read in a book somewhere, that "while a patient is *dying*, he should be *living*, until the moment he takes his last breath and dies."

He thought about this for a while and then he said: "I like that, Doctor." So I asked: "What does *living* mean to you? Maybe we can focus on that instead of being focused on your dying."

Eugene had all the answers ready about what living meant to him. He wanted to take better pictures. He wanted to go back to his dark room to develop his pictures. He wanted to listen to and tape good classical music. He wanted a really expensive watch which he never could afford. He wanted his wife and me to spend his fun money while he was alive so he could enjoy watching us do it.

We worked on his living. I told him to use a wheelchair to go to his dark room instead of walking in order to conserve his energy. We ordered catalogues on the latest photographic equipment, on classical music, on recording devices, and on expensive watches. Eugene had the time of his life buying everything he wanted. He was no longer bored, because instead of dying, he was actually living.

Three weeks later, I told Eugene I had to go to England to take a course and much as I wanted to, I could not cancel it. Will he mind it very much if I left for a week? I would ask someone to see him in my absence. He said: "Go, Doctor. Nothing will happen to me because I will not allow anything to happen while you are away." I left for England and when I came back a week later, I found out that Eugene had died the night before, in the hospital. I was sad, but it was all right. He had been living. He was comfortable. He had been doing all the things he never had the time to do while he was working. His family was ready. His wife and I on his insistence had sometimes gone to expensive French restaurants for lunch to spend his fun money.

He was in the hospital where the nurses and doctors knew what to do when death finally came. I was grateful to have been part of the last phase of Eugene's life-.

I remember Betty who was 55 years old when she was diagnosed with breast cancer. The disease progressed very rapidly and she was referred to me by her attending physician so I could help her through the last part of her life.

Frank was Betty's husband. I had never seen a more loving and devoted husband as Frank. He waited on her day and night. At night he slept on the floor beside Betty's bed so he could be awake every time she needed something. Betty also had everything that money can buy.

The hospice concept of care demands a multidisciplinary approach to terminal illness. For patients to die peacefully and painlessly, all the problems that pertain to physical, social, psychological and spiritual needs must be addressed competently and effectively. It is important also that the hospice caregivers are sensitive to the patient's and families' right to privacy.

In keeping with these tenets, and yet needing information to be of real help to the patient and members of the family, I made it a practice to look around the house for signs that would give me an idea of where they were coming from, especially in the realm of the spirit. If I saw a crucifix, I knew they were Catholic. If I saw lines from Proverbs or the Psalms, they were usually Protestants. In the case of Betty and Frank, I had been coming for three weeks and I still had no clue about anything. So one day, I casually asked: "Your name sounds Irish. Does that mean that you are Catholic?"

Frank reacted vehemently and said: "Oh, no, Doctor. We are not Catholic. In fact, we do not believe in God at all."

When Frank walked me to my car later on, I sort of apologized for asking the question. "You see," I said, "when someone is in Betty's situation, it helps sometimes if a minister or a priest would come. That is the reason why I asked."

A week later, Frank called me at 10:00 in the morning to say that something was happening to Betty. Could I come? I dropped everything and rushed to their home. Betty was actively dying, so I told Frank: "Betty is dying. Why don't you call all those who need to know so they can come right away?" He left the room to make the phone calls.

Then I did something which I had never done before in my entire career. I felt this sudden urge to kneel beside Betty's bed and as she lay dying, I whispered in her ear: "Betty, follow me." And then I made a very short act of faith, an act of love and an act of sorrow. Then I slowly said the "Our Father." I did not hear Frank come in. As I finished the prayer, I saw him standing behind me. He asked: "Doctor, do you think she heard you?" I said: "I do not know, Frank." And then he said: "I wish that she had heard you."

Betty died and, with the help of their friends, we managed to have a beautiful funeral service. In life, Frank did all the right things for Betty, and more. In death, he felt she needed a beautiful funeral even though he had said he did not believe in God, and he gave it to her.

A week later, on a Sunday, I called Frank's home to find out how he and the family were getting along. This is the bereavement follow-up, which is an important part of hospice care. His daughter answered the phone and said her father was not home. When I asked what time they were expecting him back, she said: "Haven't you heard, Doctor? After Mom's death, we all started going to church. That is where Dad is right now." God uses many ways to call His children to Him. This time, He used Betty's death.

One day I received a phone call from a gentleman who sounded like a very important executive. He sounded as if he was used to directing people and having everything done exactly the way he wanted. He asked me to see his father at the suggestion of his attending physician.

I drove to this big mansion and the gentleman (I will call him Bill) who had called met me at the door. He said, without any ceremony: "My father has cancer, and he does not know it. I do not want you to tell him. He is dying, and he does not know."

I said in reply: "I am sorry, but it is my belief that patients are entitled to know their diagnosis and their prognosis, because it is their life. They should be able to decide what to do with it. Maybe you should call another doctor who can do what you want him to do." He probably saw how unchangeable my position was, so he said it was all right for me to see his father. I went up stairs to the sick man's room.

The gentleman was 65 years old, sitting in bed because he was trying to catch his breath. As I entered the door, he looked up and said: "Doctor, I have lung cancer. They think I do not know, but I know. I am dying and I know it. They think I don't know. Just do something for me, please."

I asked him what he wanted and he said: "Please do not bring me to the hospital. I hate hospitals. Just keep me here in my son's home and let me die here." I told him that it was not as simple as that: "If I keep you here, your son will have to be your primary caregiver and I am not sure he can handle that. Let me talk to him first." I went downstairs and explained to Bill what his father wanted: keep him home and help him die at home. Can he handle that?

Bill asked: "How long, Doctor?" I said, about three to four weeks. He thought about that for a while and then he said: "He has been a good father to me, and I can sacrifice four weeks of my life. Let us keep him here."

I took care of Bernie in his son's house, but his son was his primary caregiver. It is inevitable to express love when taking care of a parent or a relative. Even just in helping to move him from bed to commode, we put our arms around the patient. Or we hold his hand in helping him with his meals. And Bill did all of these for his father.

One morning, the old man said: "Son, hold me." So Bill picked up his father and held him in his arms. His father sighed and died in his son's arms.

As soon as it happened, Bill got into his car and drove to my home to say: "Doctor, my father just died, and I am sure you would like to know. But I came here, not just to tell you that, but also to thank you for allowing me to take care of my father. You see, in our family we never say I love you. We just presume that everybody loves everybody else, and there is no need to say it. These last three weeks have enabled me to show my father how much I love him, and he died knowing I do love him. Thank you." We were both crying.

Bernie and I had become friends. Early on when I began taking care of him, he learned that I was a Catholic. He said one day: "I have something over you, Doctor. You see, my initials are BVM, exactly the same as those of the Blessed Virgin Mary." And he proudly showed me his bowling ball on which were painted in bold white letters: BVM.

12

"I want to be alive until I die"

Marianne was referred to me by her attending physician because her pain was out of control and she was very depressed. She was terminally ill with lung cancer.

I made a house call to see Marianne, and I found this very pale, emaciated lady lying in bed, very weak. As I entered her room, she said to me: "Doctor, I am dying. I am not afraid, but I would like to be alive until I die."

I was startled because those words had been written by Dr. Elisabeth Kubler-Ross in her famous book, *On Death and Dying*. And here was this dying patient saying the very same words to me. I asked her if she had read the book and she said: "No, Doctor. They are my own words. I just really want to be alive until I die." I told her that people are not all alike, so can she tell me what being alive means to her? If I knew, maybe I could try to help. She said several things: "I want to be free from pain." She had gone to medical center after medical center, physician after physician for the previous two years, and the pain would not go away.

She also said: "I want to be able to eat again." Radiation treatment and chemotherapy had caused complete loss of her appetite. She had not eaten a regular meal for months.

"I want my children to visit me every day," she said. She had seven children. "I want my grandchildren around me."

She also said: "I want to watch television and enjoy my special programs." She had been a concert pianist and she loved to listen to classical music.

I did all the things I needed to do and wrote the prescriptions for her medication, and then I left. Four days later, at eleven o'clock at night, the phone rang in my house. It was her daughter saying: "I apologize for calling you at home and so late at night, but I just felt you will be so happy to learn that my mother is completely free from pain and she cannot believe it."

Three days later, I made another house call on Marianne. There she was in a beautiful robe, sitting in front of the television set, her hair done and with makeup, and she said to me: "Doctor, I am so ashamed of myself." I asked why and she said that since my last visit she had been free from pain and she was eating like a horse. Her daughter would bring her food to her room, saying that if she needed seconds all she had to do was holler. And the daughter was barely out of the door when she would be screaming for more food. Her appetite had come back.

Her children were visiting her every day. Her grandchildren were playing around her. She was watching television. When Marianne died a month later, I said: "Thanks be to God. She had been alive until she died."

Hospice believes that a human being is not composed of just a physical body that can have disease, but that he is a composite of the physical, the social, the psychological, and the spiritual. Thus, for a patient to really die a good death, all the problems that pertain to all the components of his being have to be addressed competently and effectively. Pain is therefore not just physical pain; sometimes it is psychological pain, sometimes it is social pain, sometimes it is emotional pain, and sometimes it is spiritual pain. Sometimes it is a combination of all of these.

I had considered myself a reasonably good Catholic, but when I first heard about spiritual pain, I could not quite understand what it was, much less identify with it. Then I took care of Florence.

Florence was only 42 years old when she was diagnosed with lung cancer at its terminal stage, so she was referred to me for hospice care. After her discharge from the hospital, I took care of Florence in her home. She was relatively comfortable. I had her pain under control, her cough was not bothering her and she had nasal oxygen to help with her breathing. This state of health continued for several weeks without any major changes and so her family and the hospice team taking care of her were quite happy.

One afternoon, during a big snowstorm, her family frantically called me on the phone saying Florence needed me. Could I please come? I responded as fast as I could. When I got to her house, there was Florence screaming and groaning as if in great pain. I asked her where the pain was, but she could not tell me. She just continued to scream and groan. In desperation, and because I did not know what to do, I asked Florence if she wanted me to pray with her. She said yes, so I started to pray aloud with her. She soon quieted down and after 30 minutes, I left.

Three hours later, I received another frantic phone call from Florence's family asking me to see Florence. By this time, I had learned that Florence's life was a big mess-a man here and there, problems of all kinds, and I began to realize that what Florence was feeling was not physical pain. It was spiritual pain. She was afraid that God would not forgive the enormity of her sins and she was afraid to meet Him. I asked Florence again if I may pray with her and she consented.

This time I asked God to forgive Florence and to assure her how much He loved her and that He was waiting for her to come home to Him. I helped Florence to say some short prayers of love and contrition. She quieted down and she died peacefully within that hour. She had given me my first experience with spiritual pain. In the Catholic tradition, the Sacrament of Reconciliation (confession) and the administration of the last sacraments would provide the patient with the grace that a patient like Florence needed. (Florence was not a Catholic and this option was not possible in her case).

One of my colleagues in Hospice of Northern Virginia called frantically to say that one of his patients was at death's door. Could I please try to see her right away? I stopped everything that I was doing and rushed to the address he gave me, hoping that I would find the patient still alive. I entered the house and saw this beautifully dressed lady literally draped on her living room couch. I was surprised because what I was expecting to see was a patient who was actively dying.

Instead the lady on the couch said to me: "Doctor, I am dying. I am not afraid because I can hardly wait to see God. This life is for the birds." All I could say in reply was how beautiful she looked and how her posture on the couch reminded me of Cleopatra.

I told her further that I was glad that she was not afraid to die and that she was anxious to see God. But, I said, I would really want to make her as comfortable as possible so can she tell me what her problems were. May I try to be of help?

She said: "I am in pain." I said I would take care of that. She said she could not sleep. I said I could take care of that also. And on and on she went with symptom after symptom for which I was glad I had the answers. And then she said: "What bothers me most is I need to go to the bathroom to urinate every hour and it keeps me awake and I do not like it."

I explained to her that the tumor in her colon was pressing on her urinary bladder. The capacity of the bladder was decreased, causing her to feel the need to void every time urine accumulated. I told her that we could remedy that problem by placing a catheter. As the urine accumulated, it got drained out again and she would not feel the need to void. But, I said, most people did not like catheters, but not to worry because I would think of something else. If she liked a catheter, I would insert one. She only thought for a few seconds and then she said: "Give me a catheter, Doctor." I placed the catheter and the problem was solved.

I mention this patient because it is an example of how hospice care differs from conventional care. If Cleopatra were a patient in the hospital and she needed a catheter, the doctor would write on the chart "Insert catheter," specifying the number and the times it should be irrigated.

In hospice care, the patient's wishes are respected because the main problems that the dying have revolve around three things: *pain, loneliness, and loss of control.* My Cleopatra was in control up to the end of her life by deciding what interventions she chose to have or not to have. She died peacefully three weeks later.

13

The Woodlawn Center

Ideal hospice care is care in the patient's own home. Many studies, both in the US and England, show that the majority of patients preferred to die in their own homes, on their own bed and surrounded by people they love amid familiar things.

In-patient hospice care, however, is sometimes necessary for several reasons. One reason for admission is if the patient's symptoms are not successfully controlled in the home, then the patient is admitted into a hospice bed, whether this is in a hospital, in a nursing home, or in a hospice facility. This admission should be a short one, preferably only for two to five days.

Another reason is if the family is exhausted from taking care of the terminally ill patient and needs a respite from this difficult task. The patient is admitted into a hospice facility, not for the sake of the patient, but for the sake of the family. It is to be remembered that one of the unique features of hospice care is that the unit of care is the patient and the members of the family.

A third reason for admission is if it is absolutely impossible to provide care for the patient in the home, because of physical or other circumstances.

The home care program of Hospice of Northern Virginia was progressing well. One evening I was invited to give a talk on the concept of hospice care in one of the Protestant churches in our area. I had discussed the probable reasons why sometimes terminally ill patients cannot be cared for in the home and therefore a hospice facility is needed. Ideally, a hospice home care program should have a hospice in-patient facility to meet such necessities.

In the question and answer period, a lady in the audience got up. She said she had been informed that one of the small local high schools was going to be closed that year because of lack of enrollment. Would that high school be a good place for a hospice in-patient facility? The name of the place was Woodlawn School.

I thought over this idea during the night and early the next morning, I went to Woodlawn School to look at the building. I met the principal who was a young-looking gentleman in blue jeans and T-shirt (very unlike the school principals of my high school days who were the epitome of stern inapproachability). I explained to him why I was there and what the hospice concept was. He immediately told me that his father was dying and he could use the type of care hospice offered. He was very cooperative.

I asked him how I could go about negotiating for the building and he gave me detailed instructions about where to go and who to see. He and I walked all over the building and discussed possible changes that would convert the high school into a health care facility.

Following the principal's instructions, I went to the Arlington county board and looked for the person who was in charge. I asked him what I needed to do to ask for the Woodlawn high school building from the county board, and he said, just write us a letter. I replied that I could do that very easily. He said it might not be that easy because the deadline for making a request of the kind was 11:00 that morning. It was 9:00 a.m.

I rushed home, sat at the typewriter and wrote the letter, requesting the Arlington school board to please turn over the Woodlawn High School to Hospice of Northern Virginia to be converted into a hospice in-patient facility. I brought the letter back before the deadline.

The gentleman read the letter and then said: "This is good, but you did not tell us how much money you need to remodel the building." I was dumbfounded at this remark, because I had not expected things to go that fast. I promised him I would come back as soon as I could get the figures he wanted.

Here was a dilemma of incredible proportions. Here I was, a widow from the Philippines, a developing country, being asked how much money I needed to remodel an American high school to convert it into an in-patient facility of the Hospice of Northern Virginia. Where do you start and what do you do, especially since you are given only a few days to come up with the answers?

Advertisers in America tell consumers to "make your fingers do the walking." In other words, when in doubt, use the yellow pages of your telephone directory. Not having too many choices at the moment, I did just that.

There were hundreds of construction companies and re-modelers of buildings, both commercial and residential, all of them offering "free and quick estimates." Since I had no other criteria on which to base my choice of a builder, I chose a contractor with an Italian-sounding name, hoping that he would be Catholic and I would have at least something in common with him. The gentleman came. I explained to him what I had in mind.

I took him over to Woodlawn High School and he took some preliminary measurements and then left, promising he would give me the estimates I needed in a few days. He did as he promised. The amount was $975,000.

I wrote another letter addressed to the Arlington school board asking for $975,000 in addition to the building, so Hospice of Northern Virginia could remodel it. The school board gave us the building and the funds. God was working.

At this point, God's providence became very obvious again. One of the original members of the board of directors, who Dorothy and Pat and I decided on that cold December night, was a gentleman from our church whose name was Alton Hlavin. When friends are made in church, one never really asks what they are doing for a living or who they are. Those things do not seem to matter. As it turned out, Al was terrified of death and dying; he had never set foot in a funeral home, much less seen a dying person.

When he was elected president of the board of Hospice of Northern Virginia and he accepted the job, he was convinced that he had gone crazy. And then the miracle revealed itself We discovered that Al was assistant superintendent of schools of Northern Virginia in charge of remodeling and designing school buildings.

He was a multi-awarded architect and engineer. No wonder God gave him the job of chairman of the board of Hospice of Northern Virginia at that precise time because he would be dealing with the remodeling of Woodlawn School to make it our hospice center.

Looking back on those hectic days of planning and building a hospice facility when none of us had any experience, guidelines nor a model of what we wanted, I realize that it took a great deal of faith. But we all prayed and trusted and the in-patient facility of Hospice of Northern Virginia became a reality.

I had a friend whose name was also Jo. She was an interior designer, world class, and she volunteered to do the interiors of the facility. She asked me what color the carpet should be and of course I said, beige. Is there any other color? She was aghast and said we are not building an office. We are creating a hospice, remember? She chose a carpet in dark forest green. To complement the color, the walls had a dark green ribbon painted gracefully on them. The effect was dramatic.

One other question she asked was about the chairs in the living room. In addition to the upholstered sofa and armchairs, we needed straight-back chairs for more seating. The ones she chose were $300 each. I complained saying, I did not even have that kind of chair in my own home. She said: "Jo, these people are dying. They need the beauty and the elegance that they might have missed in their lifetime." We got the expensive chairs.

Following the St. Christopher's Hospice philosophy, we decided against the American way of having patients alone in single rooms. Instead, we too had bays of six beds each. Every bed was separated from the next with a beautiful flowered curtain in pastel colors matching the wallpaper. In the middle of each bay was a round table with a huge vase of fresh flowers and magazines of all kinds, all of them current. The facility was designed for 14 beds with provisions for six more in the future.

The facility had two sections: the administrative offices which were on the ground floor, and the patients' area which was five steps higher. The latter had its own private entrance through the front of the building, but was also accessible through the administrative area. From the donated offices in a Methodist church where HNV had been housed for almost five years, we transferred to our own home. It was a day of great rejoicing.

Over the years, HNV had undergone many changes. Its office spaces had to be expanded. In addition to the Woodlawn facility, HNV rents additional offices to accommodate its requirements in other sections of Northern Virginia. The Woodlawn Center continues to be its only in-patient facility. It still has only 14 beds, the best indication that the hospice home care program is meeting its patients' needs. Admission into a hospice bed is limited to rare cases. This is the way it should be.

From the original budget of zero, Hospice of Northern Virginia now has an annual budget of $14 million. Part of this budget is contributed annually by the community of Northern Virginia.

14

"Out of the hearts of people who care"

In January 1978, during the second year of my fellowship in medical oncology at Georgetown, I received a phone call. One of the people who had started to be interested in hospice asked me: "Jo, will you be the program director of the first annual meeting of the National Hospice Organization?" They wanted to hold the meeting in Washington, D.C., in order to attract the attention of national leaders to the importance of hospice care.

Off the top of my head, I said yes. I figured since I lived in Washington, what was one more meeting to arrange? What I did not know was that there was no National Hospice Organization, there were no funds, there was nothing. Nonetheless the first thing I did was to look for a venue for the meeting. I soon discovered that in Washington, D. C., all the major hotels are booked solid sometimes five years in advance. My first attempts were discouraging, but one group which had reserved the hotel cancelled and Shoreham Hotel became available.

The first question the hotel asked was: what is the track record of National Hospice Organization? I had to admit that it was going to be our first meeting. It must have been the prayers and the fact that my companion, a lawyer, looked very distinguished. The hotel manager reluctantly agreed to hold our event.

Now that we had a venue, we needed to put a program together, develop a mailing list, choose the speakers and contact them and attend to the myriad other details that go with a national meeting. Hospice was unknown in the US at that time. In my most optimistic estimate, an attendance of 400 persons would be realistic. We would do it classroom style and we planned everything with the hotel along those lines.

I love to see important people in a program, so I started at the top. The Secretary of Health, Education and Welfare Joseph Califano agreed to be the banquet speaker; Senator Edward Kennedy agreed to give the keynote address; and Senator Robert Dole agreed to be the luncheon speaker.

Once the program was mailed out, the phone in my office at Georgetown never stopped ringing. Before I knew it, the 400 slots were filled. I increased the number to 600, then to 800, then to 1,000 and finally to 1,200. We changed the arrangement from classroom style to theater style to accommodate everyone. It was unbelievable.

Senator Kennedy did not read his prepared speech. Instead he spoke about his father, Ambassador Joseph Kennedy who was ill and helpless for a long time. He said that they took care of him in their home and that they were fortunate because they had the necessary resources. He said that he knew that many people are unable to do what they did. Then he said the memorable words: "The hospice movement is a good movement, not because it was mandated by the federal government, nor legislated by Congress, but because it evolved out of the hearts of people who care." Thus hospice in the US began as a grassroots effort. People who cared got together and put a hospice program together in their communities. There were no funds and no guidelines but they went ahead to provide care for the dying and out of their caring, the hospice concept worked and thrived.

Secretary Califano praised the concept of hospice care and, at this meeting, announced that the federal government should get involved in the delivery of hospice care. In order to do that, he said that his office would fund a national program to determine the actual cost of hospice care compared with conventional hospital care. This program eventually became the Health Care Financing Administration (HCFA), which selected 13 programs from various parts of the US to become pilot projects on hospice care.

The first National Hospice Organization annual meeting took place in Washington, D.C., on November 8, 1978. I like to think of it as the birthplace and birth date of the hospice program in the US. The participants called the meeting "a religious experience" and, highly inspired and motivated, they returned to their communities. Full of zeal and enthusiasm, they were ready to form hospice programs. They became the grassroots out of which grew the modern hospice movement in America. Thus for many years, there were as many types of hospice programs as there were types of communities and leaders who developed them.

By 1980, the number of programs had grown from a handful to several hundred. Still, there were no guidelines, no organization manuals, no standards. The National Hospice Organization that followed the first annual meeting did not successfully meet the needs that then existed. Management was required and I was asked to be the first executive director. I refused.

I was busy taking care of cancer patients at Georgetown and being medical director of the pilot project on hospice care and of Hospice of Northern Virginia which I had helped to start. Repeatedly I refused the offer to run NHO. Then Father Healy, the president of Georgetown, called me. A few years back, he had encouraged me to establish a hospice program at Georgetown. This time, he said to me: "Jo, the hospice movement in the US needs the right kind of leadership at this point in its history. You are the right person to provide that leadership, because of your firm spiritual foundation. Take the job, put it all together and then come back to Georgetown."

I accepted the job but not before I asked the board of directors how much salary the position carried. I said I could not accept anything less than what Georgetown was paying me because I had a mortgage on the house and kids in college. The answer was: we do not care how much money you pay yourself because there is no money anyway. As part of your job, you will have to look for it yourself.

That was how I started as the first executive director of the National Hospice Organization. There was no organization really, no office and no staff. However, there was a lawsuit. Apparently NHO owed $25,000 to a management company which sued in court for payment.

The first thing to do was look for office space. Necessarily it had to be in a respectable part of metropolitan Washington. One of the most important objectives of NHO was to call the attention of national leaders to the need for hospice care.

I spent a whole day looking at office spaces, which had to be both decent and affordable, considering the zero funds of our organization. Finally I found a suite in the McLean area which met our needs. When I asked the manager if I could meet the owner of the building, he said that he was authorized to make all the decisions. There was no need to talk to the owner. I politely insisted and very reluctantly he agreed and made the appointment for me to meet the owner the following day.

The owner was one of those stern-looking gentlemen who immediately send the message not to bother him unless the matter was earthshaking. I explained to him that I found a suite of rooms in his building and I was wondering if he would allow NHO to occupy them rent-free for two years. He was shocked. "Why should I do that?" he said, gruffly. I explained to him what hospice is and that NHO was a non-profit organization, so that the rent he would waive for two years was tax-deductible. He seemed surprised by the idea and was quiet for a few minutes. Then he said: "Why don't you make it one year rent-free and, after that, sign a lease for two years?" Once again God was working things out. I signed the necessary papers and NHO had a home in McLean.

There was no staff and no money to hire anyone. Fortunately I had many friends who were only too willing to help out. For many months, we had volunteer receptionists, secretaries and administrative assistants. We looked at whatever records existed. We began to see what was going on in the various hospice programs then in operation, what potential members NHO might get and how much in membership dues might be expected. At the same time, we were dealing with lawyers on the lawsuit for nonpayment and we were making depositions. It was a very busy time but it was a good beginning.

The most pressing need was for funds, so we could hire a secretary and an individual who would be in charge of NHO memberships. Very soon, things began to fall into place. Membership dues started to come in. The lawsuit was settled amicably because the plaintiff made a tactical error. We were able to hire an executive secretary, a receptionist and a membership coordinator.

The board of directors began to play a more meaningful role. Representatives from hospice programs became more involved in our affairs. Committees to draft standards, education, training and research were formed with members from all parts of the country. State legislatures began to draft laws to govern the delivery of hospice care.

Through Health Care Financing Administration, the federal government took a greater interest in the reimbursement for hospice services by Medicare. With the help of powerful lobbyists representing the hospice movement, the US Congress started to work on legislation which eventually led to the amendment of the Social Security Act, making hospice service reimbursable by both Medicare and Medicaid.

Because of the great and urgent need for the education and training of hospice professionals, I submitted a proposal to the Kellogg Foundation for $950,000 for this purpose. Kellogg gave NHO a grant for $750,000 for education and training. The only part of the proposal that was not funded was the portion for residencies and internships in hospice care.

As executive director of NHO, I traveled to many parts of the United States. In one of those trips, the television network ABC tracked me down to invite me to a live national broadcast in "Good Morning, America" with David Hartman, at that time the most famous television anchor person. I was to debate with a congressman from California on the use of morphine to control pain in the terminally ill.

While it was a good opportunity to talk about how pain in the dying can be controlled, it was also a frightening thought. If I said the wrong things on live national television, I could very easily destroy what we in hospice had been trying to build over the past years. To make matters worse, I was going to debate with a congressman who was not a physician; therefore he and I would be talking on different planes and points of view.

Being a guest in "Good Morning, America" was intimidating enough. Someone met me at the door of the plane and whisked me in a limousine to the ABC studios in Manhattan where I was handed over to a makeup artist to prepare me for the cameras. Then I was ushered into a waiting room to wait our turn. I was very nervous, wondering what the congressman and I would debate about. I saw him rushing to the makeup artist in the next cubicle. I prayed to the Holy Spirit to help me say the right things and then it was time for our segment.

To my surprise, instead of the belligerent attitude that I was expecting, the congressman started off by saying that he will agree to whatever Doctor Magno had to say about the use of morphine to control pain in the dying. He said that he had seen many dying soldiers in Vietnam who, he believed, did not have to die in such great pain. And he proceeded to speak about his own experiences in the war, and our segment came to an end.

We did not have a debate and the message got through to the viewers that pain in the dying can be controlled by the correct use of morphine. That was all that was needed. There was no reason for my trepidation about the debate. God heard my prayers as He always does.

By September 1983, I felt that I had done what I could for NHO. The number of hospice programs in the US had reached 1,200 and they were located in each of the 50 states. I felt that I had done what Father Healy had pointed out to me when he urged me to take on the job as NHO executive director "to put it all together and then come back to Georgetown."

I quit my job. By this time, a new need had surfaced: physicians were not referring their terminally ill patients for hospice care. Many of them were, in fact hostile to the concept of hospice. Physicians are taught and trained to cure disease, to save lives, to prolong life. Hospice care is the exact opposite: do not try to cure, do not save the life, do not prolong life.

If hospice was to flourish in the US, there was an urgent need to remedy this long-held orientation of the physicians. So began to emerge the idea of an International Hospice Institute, to be based in Georgetown University, in order to educate and involve physicians in the concept of hospice care.

1944, Manila: Wedding of Josefina H. Bautista and Cesar P. Magno

1976, London: With Dame Cicely Saunders at St. Christopher's Hospice

"Out of the hearts of people who care" 77

1981, Washington D.C.: After taking oath as an American Citizen

1981, Washington D.C.: Working for hospice legislation with Ann Dailey and Marcie Corbett through Senator Jennings Randolph

"Out of the hearts of people who care"

1984, Arlington VA.: At Home on Military Road

1983, Arlington VA: With only daughter Nanette and sons Carlo, Manolo, and Mario (seated); Jose, Vicente, and Cesar Jr. (standing)

1987, Detroit MI.:
With the hospice staff of the Henry Ford Health System

"Out of the hearts of people who care"

1994, Detroit MI: Accepting the Humanitarian Award from Gail Warden, President of the Henry Ford Health System

1997, Arlington VA: Addressing Capital Hospice (formerly Hospice of Northern Virginia) supporters at 20th Anniversary Gala with George Shafran, emcee for the evening

1987, Washington D.C.: With Philippines Ambassador Pelaez and Mrs. Edith Pelaez

1988, Tondo District Compound, Manila, Philippines: With Mother Teresa and the Missionaries of Charity and sister Betts Razon

15

Involving the physicians

While the hospice movement in the US had come of age by 1983 and there were hospice programs in every state and giant steps had been made by the US Congress to pass legislation which made hospice services reimbursable by Medicare and Medicaid, one big problem persisted: the lack of interest on the part of the medical profession in the hospice concept of care.

After I gave a talk in one of the hospitals in Northern Virginia, one physician angrily commented: "How dare you say that we physicians in America do not know how to manage pain?" On another occasion, I was asked to give a talk on hospice care at the annual meeting of the staff physicians of a large New York hospital. I was at the head table and the president of the medical staff was seated on my right. I tried to make small talk by asking him how much he knew about hospice care. He said: "I know all about it already. In fact, one of my nurses recently got sick and hospice took care of her. They held her hand and she died." I did not argue with him.

After the presentation, however, he approached me and apologized saying that he was wrong. He thought that hospice was nothing but handholding and he could do that too.

Attitudes such as these, added to the appeal made by hospice providers from all over the country to make physicians refer their terminally ill patients for hospice care, made imperative the creation of an organization to address this problem. In late 1983, the International Hospice Institute (IHI) was founded. The head was the chief of medical oncology at Georgetown University Hospital, and the members were a doctor from Poland, a doctor of American-Japanese ancestry, a distinguished practitioner from Johns Hopkins University Hospital and myself. The IHI was registered as a private, not for profit organization with one purpose: to involve the medical profession in the delivery of hospice care.

The first step was to create a task force which would look at why physicians were so indifferent to the concept of hospice care. The task force was composed of university presidents, presidents of medical societies, and outstanding practitioners in the metropolitan Washington area. The report of the task force stated that the reason for the lack of interest of physicians in hospice care was ignorance. The great majority of doctors did not understand what hospice care is and how it would affect their practice.

The recommendation to remedy this problem included two points: to develop an annual symposium on the concept of hospice care designed specifically for physicians, using only the most highly respected authorities in the field of hospice care as faculty; and to form an Academy of Hospice Physicians to provide doctors with a forum where they can share and exchange information and provide peer support for one another. The first board meeting of IHI was held on March 19, 1984, the feast of Saint Joseph, in Arlington, Virginia. The first annual hospice symposium on hospice care was held in July 1985. It was attended by only 25 physicians, but it was a beginning.

In succeeding years, attendance at the annual symposium grew by leaps and bounds. The symposium was held in places which were not glamorous five-star hotels, but family-type resorts so that the hospice physicians of the time, most of whom were volunteers, could bring their families without spending a fortune. The atmosphere at those meetings was friendly and warm. One participant commented that while at the professional organization meetings, you hardly made friends with anyone, the IHI symposia made you feel a sense of camaraderie, a sense of belonging.

Dr. Andrew Billings of Harvard attended the second symposium in Estes Park, Colorado, with his whole family. Early one morning he was sitting in the living room of the rustic hotel where the symposium was being held. He was trying to write his talk on a yellow pad paper while minding his four-year-old son. He said to me: "When I started to practice hospice at Massachusetts General Hospital, people thought I was crazy. I also thought I was the only one who was crazy enough to do that. I felt isolated and alone. Then I come here and I discover that I am not crazy after all. There are other physicians who feel as strongly as I do about the care of the terminally ill patient. It is a great feeling."

Sentiments like those expressed by Andy Billings led to the formation of the Academy of Hospice Physicians (AHP) in July 1988. I had sent letters to 1,000 physicians from all over the US, using the directory of ASCO (American Society of Clinical Oncologists) asking them to join in the new organization. I received 125 responses, and these became the founding members of the AHP.

I had said to myself that in five years AHP could have 500 members, I would consider it a big success. Miracle of miracles, in three years we had more than 500 members and the number was increasing at a fast rate. The response was very gratifying because it showed that physicians were beginning to take notice and understand the concept of hospice care. The AHP membership also swelled the number of participants of the IHI annual symposium on hospice care. By 1995, more than 400 registrants attended the meeting in Vancouver.

Other sites of the IHI symposium included the Royal Lancaster Hotel in London, the Georgetown University Conference Center in Washington, D.C., the Hyatt Regency in Vancouver, B.C., the Choo-Choo Hotel in Chattanooga, Tennessee, and others. The hospice symposium designed for physicians had come of age.

In the meantime, the Academy of Hospice Physicians continued to grow, having been born on faith and a prayer. I had asked Angela Cyr, Ed.D., if she would be the volunteer executive director of AHP until we could have enough funds to pay her a salary. She graciously accepted and, under her guidance, the organization took shape. Various committees were formed, election of officers and board members took place every year, membership dues were structured and implemented, and the AHP expanded its horizons. However, as in all important things in life, growth is often accompanied by changes-in attitudes, in spirit, and in purpose.

In 1995, at the IHI symposium in Vancouver, the AHP board of directors decided that the AHP should change its name to American Academy of Hospice/Palliative Medicine (AAHP) and that it would hold its annual meeting separately and independently of IHI, its parent organization. These changes were effected in June 1996. A management expert replaced Dr. Angela Cyr, the first executive director, the offices were expanded, and the staff members increased.

IHI was undergoing some changes also. In 1989, the World Health Organization through Dr. Jan Stjernsward, its chief of cancer and palliative medicine, made an appeal to the West to share their expertise in the care of the terminally ill with the rest of the world. Statistics had shown that in spite of the great strides made in the management of pain, 75% of people who were dying were still dying in pain. This was especially true in the developing nations of the world. In response to this appeal, IHI added a third goal to its mission: to help bring the concept of hospice care to the developing countries of the world.

At the Vancouver IHI Symposium when the Academy of Hospice Physicians made the decision to break away from IHI, its parent organization, I thought that the mission of IHI had been accomplished and the time had come for it to fold up its tent and close shop. I felt no anger nor resentment, because I looked on the AHP as a child which had grown and was trying its wings for the first time. But people in IHI felt very strongly that IHI must continue to exist because there were other things that needed to be done.

A group of doctors attending the symposium called me on the phone to drag me out of bed because "we needed to talk." We sat in one of the plazas of Vancouver, the night was beautiful and a gentle breeze was blowing. It was 2:00 in the morning and the group decided that IHI should now focus on its new third mission of bringing the concept of hospice care to the developing countries of the world. I agreed but only on the condition that we would appoint a committee of twelve who will pray for guidance, so that whatever IHI will do next is not motivated by personal ambitions but only by the good of mankind. On that note we adjourned the impromptu meeting and everyone went to bed.

After the Vancouver meeting, dialogue continued on this new mission of IHI, and prayers continued to be offered. One of the men in hospice/palliative care that I admire most in the world is Dr. Derek Doyle, then medical director of St. Columba's Hospice in Scotland. The author of many books on hospice/palliative care, Doctor Doyle travels all over the world to lecture on the subject of terminal illness.

Many years earlier, I mustered enough courage to ask him to give a presentation at one of the IHI symposium or physicians and he graciously accepted my invitation. We became good friends. He used to be a medical missionary in South Africa for many years, so he combined medical ideas and spiritual insights in the most natural and graceful manner.

Since IHI was going to focus on a global mission of bringing hospice to the developing countries of the world, I said to myself: wouldn't it be wonderful if Doctor Doyle would lead this important undertaking? I had heard that he would be retiring as medical director of St. Columba's Hospice in the middle of that year, so there was some chance that he might give the offer serious consideration. As usual, I prayed and then I called Derek.

He would be on a lecture tour in Canada but he said he could meet me in Toronto at this *fancy* hotel where he was staying. I flew to Toronto and I told him I wanted to have the nicest lunch we could find so we could talk. I was planning to treat him to lunch in a manner befitting the celebrity that he was.

I explained the idea of the new direction that IHI was taking and asked: can he help? We talked for an hour and then he said: "Jo, I will take the job for a year and a half, but only on one condition, and that is you and I are going to assume this big undertaking in thanksgiving for all the blessings that God has showered on you and me, and for no other reason." He had expressed the very thoughts that were in my heart. My only regret was he insisted on paying for the fancy lunch to which I had wanted to treat him.

In June 1996, the IHI board of directors changed the name of IHI to the International Hospice Institute and College (IHIC). Dr. Derek Doyle became the president of the college while I continued to be president of IHIC. The necessary changes in by-laws were made including the change in the mission statement. The membership of IHI became truly international.

In 1997, I felt the need to stay more and more in the Philippines because I wanted to use the country, which is my homeland, as a testing ground for how a new concept in health care, like hospice, can be successfully introduced. I created a management committee to be responsible for the day-to-day management of IHIC, and asked Dr. Roger Woodruff, oncologist, author and an expert on hospice/palliative care from Melbourne, Australia to head it. He agreed and I was grateful.

By 1998, I made the decision to retire from IHIC because being in the Philippines caused me to be too far away from the scene of the action, and it was not fair to the board of IHIC for me to be an absentee president. At IHIC's board meeting in Montreal in 1998, I was made president emeritus of IHIC. The management committee was changed to an executive committee, co-chaired by Roger Woodruff and Derek Doyle. I know that IHIC is in the best of hands.

16

Hospice for profit

I had been invited to give the keynote address at the Texas Hospice Organization annual meeting. At the luncheon, I was surprised to see so many physicians with a nametag which said Family Hospice. It will be recalled that one of the early problems of the hospice movement in America was the lack of involvement of the medical profession in the delivery of hospice care. Professional organizations would send invitations and all kinds of inducements to physicians to attend a meeting on hospice care, and it was a lucky day if one or two doctors appeared. And here at the Texas Hospice Organization, there were at least 20 physicians, all of them wearing the same identification: Family Hospice.

Of course I was pleased and at the same time intrigued with this new turn of events and I wanted to know how it all came about. That was when I met Dr. Alex Peralta for the first time. He was the medical director of Family Hospice, a for-profit hospice home care program with main offices in Dallas, Texas.

Many years before, when I was developing Hospice of Northern Virginia, I tried to look for a hospital with a good reputation which would give us six hospital beds which we could convert into hospice beds. The most highly recommended hospital for the purpose was Northern Virginia Doctors' Hospital. I went to see the administrator, and his opening comment to me was: "Doctor, we are a for-profit hospital and we are not apologizing for that. We are for-profit because we want to give our patients the best care possible and maintain the best hospital surroundings for them. That is why we watch our expenses and our revenue so that we can do all the things we want to do and still remain operational and highly efficient."

Our negotiations did not push through because Hospice of Northern Virginia was given an old high school building, the Woodlawn School, which we remodeled into a hospice in-patient facility. But I never forgot the rationale for a for-profit health care provider which the administrator of the Northern Virginia

Doctors' Hospital helped me to understand. And it was with that understanding that I came to know Family Hospice better.

Alex Peralta had great dreams and aspirations about providing the highest quality of hospice home care in their part of the world, and he believed that the only way to do that is to provide their patients with intensive physician attention. Therefore, Family Hospice must have physicians on the staff who would make house calls as often as necessary and they must be highly trained in all aspects of hospice care.

Alex had talked to the owners of Family Hospice, a young couple who are extremely Christ-centered, about how it might be good for Family Hospice to ask Doctor Magno to be consultant to Family Hospice on the training of their physicians. Rocky and Carol Reese, Alex's bosses, agreed to the idea so they planned their strategy very carefully. I was going to be flown to Dallas and the three of them would pick me up at the airport and take me to lunch at the most expensive restaurant in Dallas, and then we could talk.

Everything went wrong. Rocky brought his brand-new vehicle to pick me up. It was a Chevy Suburban, the latest model with all the trimmings, bright red, sparkling clean. Except that I was wearing a suit with a slim skirt, which obviously was not designed for a Suburban and so it took a lot of time and effort before I could get into the vehicle. But we did get to the fancy restaurant where reservations had been made.

Alex was wearing a dark blue blazer and a white shirt, but he had on a pair of blue jeans. It was a Saturday. The maitre d' took one look and, with the most abject apology, told us that Alex could not be allowed into the restaurant because it was company policy. He even added that Mick Jagger wearing blue jeans had come to the restaurant and they had to turn him away. Dilemma.

After we had all become friends, they told me that they had never tried so hard to impress a guest and they were falling on their faces every inch of the way. The maitre d' found a solution. He would smuggle us into a small private dining room where no one would see Alex's blue jeans. And that was what he did. We had a fabulous lunch, and it marked the beginning of my association with Family Hospice.

Family Hospice started with two patients who promptly died thus immediately reducing their patient census to zero. Alex had been in private practice as an internist when Rocky and Carol Reese recruited him for the position of full time medical director of Family Hospice. Alex is a Catholic, a fourth degree Knight of Columbus, married with three grown daughters. He was a pharmacist before he went to medical school.

My role as consultant to Family Hospice on education and research was to work with Alex on the training of the staff, and to develop education and research activities which Family Hospice could share with the community that it serves. In time, Family Hospice grew to cover much of Texas, Oklahoma and New Mexico. Most of the work I did could be accomplished by phone or by mail, but I did go to Texas every three or four months to conduct courses and meet with the staff. These visits were some of the most memorable experiences in my life, because they evolved more into spiritual exercises than teaching sessions. I attribute this to Alex's own belief that true hospice care can be as good only as the attitude of the caregivers and the basic philosophy of the organization, that is, to serve the patients who are brought to Family Hospice in the best way possible.

I was chatting with one of Family Hospice's medical directors, Waddan Nassar, who was from Oklahoma and he was telling me why he was so loyal to Family Hospice. He said he had been taking care of a patient for almost a month. The man's pain was so severe that the doctor had been using unbelievable amounts of morphine to relieve the pain. At some point, he noticed that more than $25,000 had gone into pain medication alone, so he consulted Alex and asked if he should give up on the patient's pain. Alex's answer: "Never. We will continue to keep the patient pain-free regardless of how much it costs." This extraordinary commitment to the care of patients has endeared Family Hospice to me.

There are many hospice programs in the US, which are not for profit, and sometimes they look down on for-profit hospices like Family Hospice as though they were second-class. If what the administrator of the Northern Virginia Doctors' Hospital told me is true, that institutions which are for profit can be very highly efficient and they can render better service to their constituents because they watch their revenues and expenses very carefully, then I am all for having for-profit hospices.

Family Hospice is such a model. With good management and a very caring staff who are kept up to date in education and training, Family Hospice grew to have a patient census from zero to 1,000 patients a day. At one point, it had more than 200 physicians on staff looking after their patients. These physicians were sent to conferences in the US and abroad at the expense of Family Hospice, and they participate as faculty in the training sessions for staff and the community that Alex and I developed. This is the kind of maturity that I am hoping and praying for all hospice programs to have regardless of whether they are for profit or not for profit.

17

The move to Michigan

After we lost our home on Military Road as a consequence of the Marcos dictatorship which caused many businesses in the Philippines, including ours to collapse, I moved in with my son, Mario, until I could have a better idea of what I wanted to do with my life.

One beautiful fall day in Washington, D.C., I received an unexpected phone call from Peg McCuistion. She was the executive director of the Hospice of Southeastern Michigan, the first hospice program in Michigan.

What was the call about? During my tenure as executive director of the National Hospice Organization from 1980 to 1983, the number of hospice programs in the US had grown to an unbelievable number of almost 1,200 programs. Many of these programs evolved "out of the hearts of people who care." Most of them were volunteer programs. They had something in common: because hospice was a new concept in the US the majority of the programs that were formed depended on the type of leaders in the communities where they were established. There was still no legislation, and there were no guidelines, but hospices were formed to meet the specific needs of the people they were going to serve.

Hospice of Southeastern Michigan (HSEM) was an example. Michigan is automobile country, and there are labor unions, which act as the guardians of the rights of the automobile workers. When the concept of hospice became known in the US, it became natural for the United Auto Workers (UAW) to demand that hospice care be included in the benefits package for their members. At this time, hospice was looked upon as in-patient care, because of its origin at St. Christopher's Hospice, and also because of the Georgetown University/Blue Cross/Blue Shield Pilot project on Hospice Care which consisted of six beds at the Washington Home for Incurables.

Fourteen hospitals in Detroit and the suburbs were providing health care services for auto workers when this demand for hospice benefits was made by the

UAW. These hospitals met and discussed the demands of the UAW and how to meet these demands. They had two choices: each hospital will develop its own hospice program or they will pool their resources together to form one hospice program to serve all the UAW members serviced by all 14 hospitals. The choice was to pool their resources together and form one hospice program for all the UAW members in the region.

One facility, the Rehabilitation Center of Southeastern Michigan, had an unoccupied second floor. Hospice of Southeastern Michigan rented this entire floor to convert it into an in-patient facility with 24 beds. A search for an executive director was made and Peg McCuistion of Austin, Texas, was hired to put the program together. As executive director of NHO at the time, I was one of the guests at the inauguration, so the program was familiar to me. The 14 area hospitals contributed a specific amount for which they were assessed to get the program off the ground. It was a spectacular success. The year was 1982.

Since hospice was a new concept in the US, reimbursement for hospice services by both government and private insurers was still a great unknown. The US government had launched the Health Care Financing Administration (HCFA) Research Project to determine the actual cost of hospice care as opposed to conventional care at the end of life, and the US Congress was working on legislation which would require Medicare and Medicaid to reimburse for hospice services.

Meanwhile, Blue Cross/Blue Shield of Michigan was asking its own questions because many of its subscribers were demanding the inclusion of hospice care in their covered services. To find its own answers, BC/BS of Michigan made Hospice of Southeastern Michigan a pilot project by giving HSEM a grant of one million dollars for one year. HSEM would document the actual cost of hospice care in an in-patient facility so it could be compared to conventional care in an acute care hospital. It was a great year for HSEM.

Patients were brought to the HSEM facility and excellent care was provided. Patients could stay for as long as needed. Families were grateful because patients died without pain and hospice provided bereavement counseling for the family members. The newspapers printed story after story about this new type of care. A red rose placed on the bed of the patient who had died and the bed kept unoccupied for 24 hours, in loving memory of the one who had passed away, caught the imagination of the public. Hospice care had come of age in Michigan.

Then in 1984, the US Congress passed the amendment to the Social Security Act mandating that Medicare and Medicaid pay for hospice services. A stipulation was included, however, requiring that hospice care be provided in the patient's own home which should comprise 80% of the total number of days of care. Only 20% of the total number of days of care can be in-patient care. HSEM had been providing 100% in-patient care because that was how the program was conceived and developed. It was a big dilemma because the community of Southeastern Michigan had seen hospice care as in-patient care in a facility with the terminally ill patient allowed to stay for an unlimited number of days.

That was the reason for Peg McCuistion's call. She had heard that the International Hospice Institute (IHI) had been formed and that one of its main purposes is the education of physicians in the concept of hospice care. As president of IHI, could I come to Michigan to talk to physicians in the state? They need to be encouraged to send their patients for whom cure of disease was no longer possible. Can we start hospice care all over again as home care, with only 20% of the care being in the facility? It was a simple enough request and I figured that three to four months stay in Michigan would accomplish the purpose.

My youngest son, Manny, was at that time a resident physician at Wayne State University in Michigan. He was sharing a two-bedroom apartment which belonged to the university with a friend from the Philippines, also a resident physician. Both of them invited me to stay with them. I came with two suitcases of clothes, thinking that these could easily meet my needs for my brief stay in Michigan.

Over the phone, Peg McCuistion told me they did not have enough money to pay me a good salary. Will that affect my coming? Of course not. Then she asked: what title can they give me? I remember saying: "Choose a title that does not mean anything, so that I can be free to do whatever is needed." We all settled for the title of Director of Community Relations.

This was my introduction to Michigan. Hospice people from any part of the world are famous for their warmth, friendliness and generosity, and these qualities are what make them the best caregivers wherever they are. The staff of HSEM from the executive director to the janitors and cleaning ladies were outstanding in every way possible. I can only look back on those days with HSEM as among the happiest in my life.

We worked very hard and, before I knew it, the four months that I had given myself were over. I knew I was going to stay. I moved out of the Wayne State University residents' quarters and found a three-bedroom apartment close to HSEM. I decided to move the IHI office from its temporary home in Georgetown to Michigan so I could have better control. My life had begun to shape up; the job at HSEM gave me enough leeway to do IHI work in addition to being Director of community relations of HSEM. And I was happy.

The BC/BS grant to HSEM had run out. Funds were needed to complement the income from its HSEM's home care and the fewer in-patient beds. One of the hospice nurses, Ginny Fitzgerald, told me in December 1984 that she knew prominent people in the community. She said she could help me hold a black tie dinner to raise funds for HSEM. Almost single-handedly, Ginny organized some of the wealthy people in Detroit and suburbs. We held a black tie dinner in April 1985 and raised $55,000 out of that one night event.

More than just raising funds, however, the black tie dinner brought the movers and shakers of the community into involvement with HSEM. In late 1985, I decided to organize a women's committee for hospice care so that Ginny need not work all by herself to set up the fund-raising events. Bud Barlow was one of the gentlemen volunteers of HSEM. He was an insurance executive and his wife, Pat, became the first president of the Women's Committee of HSEM.

Under Pat Barlow's leadership, the board of directors of HSEM recognized the women's committee on hospice care and it became a separate entity with its own legal personality. Subsequently, it decided that the other hospice programs, which had started to form in Michigan should become part of this women's committee, help in setting up the fund-raising events, and share in the proceeds.

Today the Women's Committee on Hospice Care has evolved to one of the most prestigious and highly respected organizations in Southeastern Michigan. Annually it raises more than $250,000 and this amount is distributed among the member hospice programs in the community to enable them to provide hospice care to everyone who needs it, regardless of ability to pay. In addition to the fund-raising activities, we held educational symposia each year to educate physicians and the general public on the concept of hospice care. We launched research activities, among them was the application of the hospice concept to nursing home care. It was a busy time, a time for growth. And sometimes growth makes changes necessary. Peg McCuistion had suffered a mild heart attack and she needed to take it easy. The board of directors of HSEM asked me to take her place, but my answer was no. I knew that I could no longer do that kind of back-breaking work. However I said I would continue doing what I was doing, being director of community relations and directing education, research and development, for the program.

Then, once again, God intervened in my life. Henry Ford Hospital was one of the 14 area hospitals providing health care services to the United Auto Workers. Its head of medical oncology, Dr. Robert O'Bryan, was consequently sitting as a member of the board of directors of HSEM. One day, he talked to me and said: "For the past 12 years, I had been trying to develop a hospice program at Henry

Ford Hospital, but I never could succeed. Why don't you help me do it? Maybe they will listen to you." I said I would try.

18

Henry Ford Hospital Hospice

Henry Ford Hospital is a historical landmark in Detroit, Michigan. Having invented the Model T-Ford, which revolutionized the transportation industry of America and the world, Henry Ford built the hospital to provide health care services for the employees of the Ford Motor Company. At the end of each year, Mr. Ford would ask the hospital management how much money the hospital needed, and he wrote a check to cover the entire amount. The Ford employees had the best health care that money could buy.

The Henry Ford Hospital over the years evolved into a world-class tertiary care hospital of 1,000 beds. Patients from all over Michigan were brought to the hospital for the most advanced medical and surgical treatments which their own community hospitals could not provide. Subsequently, it became necessary for the hospital to create satellites in order to better serve the patients in the various areas of the community. Some of these satellites were community hospitals; some of them were sophisticated clinics with all the specialties represented on the staff. Major surgical cases were referred to the main hospital in Detroit.

Into this complex organization, Dr. Robert O'Bryan invited me to help develop a hospice program in February 1987. Dr. O'Bryan is an oncologist who not only practiced his profession with the greatest competence, but also cared passionately for his patients. He believed that patients should be in the care of their physicians, not only when their disease could be cured, but up to the last moment of life. He was a hospice physician at heart.

At that time, Henry Ford Hospital had a home care program, through which patients continued to be provided with care in their homes after discharge from the hospital. It was a practical way of complying with the requirement of insurance providers to limit the number of hospital stays to a minimum without depriving the patients of the care they needed. Patients under the home care program were usually not terminally ill; they were acute care patients who had to undergo hospitalization for surgical intervention or intensive medical treatment. Home care services were reimbursable by both government and private insurers, including Medicare and Medicaid.

I started my work with Henry Ford Hospital as a consultant for two days a week. I was not sure how to approach the need for a hospice program in this sophisticated health care system.

Because of my training as an oncologist, I was assigned to the division of medical oncology, of which Dr. O'Bryan was chief of division. I was fortunate because Dr. O'Bryan succeeded in enlisting the cooperation of one of the system's vice presidents, Alan Case, to help me understand the system and how it worked.

In comparing the two assignments, i.e., the Georgetown University Hospital pilot project on hospice care and the Henry Ford Hospital hospice program, there were two major differences. The Georgetown project happened in 1977 when hospice was unknown in the United States; at that time I was all alone in facing the challenge. The Henry Ford Hospital project happened ten years later, in 1987, when hospice care was almost a part of the health care system of the US and it was much easier for hospital administrators to understand the need for hospice care when cure of disease was no longer possible. Since hospice is both humanitarian and cost-effective, it had its own appeal in various levels.

Working with Alan Case, I examined the existing Henry Ford Hospital home care program. Did it have elements that could be expanded or adapted to the hospice concept of care? If so, how can this expansion or adaptation be made without any major administrative or financial changes? We were looking out for hospice care's three major components: care in the patient's home; multidisciplinary care; and reimbursement for hospice home care services by Medicare and Medicaid and private insurance companies.

Working with the Henry Ford Hospital home care management staff under the guidance of Alan Case, we soon identified a commonality of purpose. Patient care can be provided in the patient's home; a multi-disciplinary team can provide care; and existing reimbursement policies would pay for hospice home care.

A major obstacle came up. One of Henry Ford Hospital's satellites is Cottage Hospital, which is located in Grosse Pointe, an affluent community in Detroit. A community hospital of 100 beds, it had been providing excellent health care services to the community for years and years. Because of its superior standard of service, Cottage Hospital was one of the first hospitals which developed its own hospice program, complying with all the regulations that covered the formation of hospices, including certificate of need, Medicare and Medicaid certification and so on. The Cottage Hospital Hospice Program was a small program which was adequate for its patient population.

With this situation of having a Henry Ford Hospital satellite already with its own hospice program, could Henry Ford Hospital still apply for a hospice certificate of need, Medicare certification, licensure as a hospice program, without duplicating efforts and documentation? Many months of debate between Cottage Hospital and Henry Ford Hospital examined this issue until a consensus was arrived at: the Cottage Hospital hospice program would be the Henry Ford Hospital hospice program. Its offices would be housed in Detroit near the Henry Ford Hospital, but its satellite office at Cottage Hospital in Grosse Pointe would continue. The director of the Cottage Hospital Hospice Program, Ms. Sondra Seeley would be the executive director of the Henry Ford Health System hospice program. Two staff oncologists, Dr. Leslie Bricker and Dr. Joseph Anderson volunteered to be co-medical directors of the hospice program.

Dr. Cicely Saunders, founder of the modern hospice movement, had always stressed that for a hospice program to succeed in its mission of providing hospice care to terminally ill patients, it must have a tripod consisting of: education, research and patient care. Education is necessary to keep the staff well trained and knowledgeable about the latest information regarding the care of the dying; research is needed to discover better methods and techniques in the care of the dying patient and the members of the family; and patient care is the application of all these for the benefit of patients and families.

In keeping with these mandates, we offered educational opportunities, not only for hospice staff and volunteers, but also for the community at large. Some of these educational activities were held in cooperation with the International Hospice Institute so we were able to bring in faculty from other parts of the US and overseas. To supplement revenue from Medicare and Medicaid and private insurers, we held fund-raising benefits. Patient families gave donations to the hospice program as a sign of their gratitude. In other words, development became an important part of the hospice program's priorities.

Two years after I joined Henry Ford Hospital at the invitation of Dr. Robert O'Bryan to help develop the Henry Ford Hospital Hospice Program, I became a full time employee with the title of Director of Hospice Education, Research and Development of the Henry Ford Health System. It was from this position that I retired in December 1995 in order to focus my attention on how to bring the concept of hospice care to the developing countries of the world. I wanted to start with my own country, the Philippines.

19

My son Mario

In 1948, my husband and I were in New York City to pursue post-graduate training in internal medicine at New York University Hospital. As I mentioned earlier in other chapters, I had accompanied my father for brain tumor surgery at Johns Hopkins University Hospital in Baltimore, and my husband met us there before my father left to go back to the Philippines. It was an exciting time for us to be in the United States because we were young and full of youthful ambitions. We had three sons by this time, and the youngest was only three months old. We left all of them in the care of my sister-in-law in my mother-in-law's big home in Nueva Ecija.

There are many Catholic churches in New York City and my husband and I used to make the rounds of all of them. On his part, it was probably just to humor me. At one of the shrines to the Blessed Mother, there was a statue of Saint Bernadette. I loved going to this particular church to pray to Our Lady, asking her to please give me a daughter because I already had three sons and it would be nice to have a baby girl. I promised her that if she granted my request, I would call the baby girl Maria Bernadette. And so my girlish prayers went day after day.

I did get pregnant and I was so sure I would have a daughter. I bought all kinds of pretty pink baby girl outfits. Training in the hospital finished in July and the baby was due in early August, so my husband and I decided to be back in the Philippines for my delivery. The reason for this decision was the fact that, in the Philippines, a mother is allowed to stay in the hospital for as long as she wants, all the time being pampered by many nurses and relatives. In the efficient American way, a mother is expected to take care of herself the day after the delivery.

I had the baby a week after we arrived in Manila on August 7, and it was a boy. We named him Mario as I had promised Our Lady.

I cannot explain it but Mario was different, even as an infant. At work as the school physician in a Catholic school, I was thinking of Mario a lot. His big smile and something about him that made you love him in a very special way. I could hardly wait to go home so I could hold him in my arms. He drew me in a way I cannot explain.

Of his first five years I do not have any unusual recollection, except that he was a very bright little boy. When the time came for him to go to school, Mario went very, very reluctantly with a great deal of crying. He did not want to go. It became so bad that every morning, he would develop a fever and he would have to stay home because of the fever. My husband and I thought about all these and decided that he was not ready for school, and that missing one year out of his whole lifetime was better than having a neurotic child. So Mario stayed home and resumed classes the next year. He was ready by that time.

In school Mario again was different. He went to the Ateneo de Manila, a private school run by the Jesuits where most of the sons of affluent families studied. The school uniform for grade school was short khaki pants and a white shirt with the Ateneo coat of arms on the breast pocket. Because of the uniform, Mario was dressed like all the other boys, but he insisted on a pair of black shoes which were "poor." He wore the same pair until they were completely worn out, and then he would ask me to buy the same pair again and again. I used to describe him then, not really knowing what I was saying, as being "out of this world." Little did I know how well I was characterizing him.

The Ateneo had a chapel for the grade school boys. Mario went to the chapel early in the morning to "visit Jesus," he said. One day he came home very sad and quiet. I asked him what was wrong and he said: "I feel so sorry for Jesus. When we all go home after class, He would be sorry to see us all leave, but He will be looking forward to the following morning so He would see us again. And then the next day, out of many hundreds of boys, only a few go to the chapel to visit Him. He must be so disappointed and sad." Mario was probably only eight or nine years old at time, but he already carried in his heart the sorrow of Jesus for the indifference of men.

One day I asked him: "What do you say to Jesus when you visit Him?" He said: "Nothing special. Sometimes I tell Him about the maids if they made me a hot dog sandwich for my snack. They already know that I hate hot dog sandwiches, but I eat it anyway."

My other children rode in a chauffeur-driven car everywhere they went. In the Philippines, you do not have to be very rich to have a car and a driver. Mario insisted on going by bus or any public transportation. He said he loved to see the other people going about their way, and he would be wondering what their lives were all about.

One day, he asked: "Why are there so many people, Mommy?" I said probably because each one has a purpose for his own existence. God created people and often times this purpose is achieved with the help of some other person.

One of my sisters, Lucila, loved Mario with a passion. She used to say she was almost terrified every time Mario asked her a question, because it would almost always be something very deep and profound for which she felt she had no correct answer.

Mario loved to draw and paint. Every time it was Parents' Day at the Ateneo, his teachers would proudly show me his drawings that were exhibited on the walls of the classroom. I did not give too much importance to these drawings because children do them all the time. But one day, Mario painted in oil a Madonna and child, a little girl and her doll. He submitted it to an art competition sponsored by the Shell Company. I saw it as the first outward indication of his great love for the Blessed Mother, a love which marked his whole life. The painting won first prize, and the Shell Company kept it for future use in their brochures. Then I knew that my son was a talented artist.

When Mario was 13 years old in high school, he did an oil painting of the Blessed Mother. This time it was of Our Mother of Perpetual Help, mostly in gold paint. He placed a real crown of gold on both the Mother and the Son. He carried this painting with him everywhere he lived in later years, including the United States.

Mario went to Mass every day. He was an exemplary student and he collected all the gold medals for excellence in almost every subject. Before the Ateneo years, he went to a school run by the Sisters of St. Paul. From then on, in every commencement exercise each year, he got so many medals that I had to go to the stage many times to pin them on him.

He also loved to read and to write. Since we are a big family, he had many first cousins of all ages. We had family reunions several times a year when the whole clan would troop to my sister Lucila's home in Pampanga and stay for two or three days. For these occasions, Mario wrote the script of a play out of the familiar fairy tales. He was producer, director and stage manager all rolled into one, with his siblings and cousins acting out the characters. It was great fun for everyone.

In high school at the Ateneo, Mario had Father Thomas Green, S.J., as his spiritual director. Under Father Green, Mario probably grew into his maximum potential in terms of his spiritual life. His favorite friends were Teresa of Avila and John of the Cross. He read spiritual books under the guidance of Father Green, and since he knew I was very busy, he would give me a book and say:

"Just read this chapter." So in his own way, he was transmitting to me what Father Green had helped him understand.

Many years later, when Father Green visited us in our home in Arlington, Virginia, I told him that Mario was my spiritual director, and Father Green teased him by saying: "Mario, you are practicing without a license."

When I left for the United States in 1969, Mario was in undergraduate premedicine at the Ateneo. He was very happy. His grades were very good, he was a leader in his class, and he had everything going for him, including a spiritual director of the caliber of Father Green. When the US approved my status in 1972 as permanent resident, my two youngest sons followed me to the US. He called me up and asked if he may continue to stay in the Philippines because he was really happy where he was. I said yes.

One year later he called and said he was coming over also. I wondered what brought on the change of heart, but I did not really ask. And then he explained that he was imagining me, his mother, doing all the cooking, cleaning and laundry for everyone because his two young siblings did not know how to do these. He felt sorry for me so he decided to leave all the happy days at the Ateneo, his friends and Father Green so he could help me with the housework.

Mario was eligible for medical school when he joined us in the United States. But he decided not to even try to gain admission into any medical school in spite of his burning desire to be a doctor. I asked him why and his answer was simple. He had come to the US to help me with the housework. If he went to medical school, it would probably be in another state, and that would defeat the very purpose of his joining us. He opted to work for a master's degree in counseling at Catholic University because that would be the closest to being a psychiatrist, which he had wanted to be in the first place.

Before Mario joined us in the US, he had asked me to go to Berryville Monastery in Virginia, take pictures of the place, and describe to him the atmosphere of the monastery. I did so. He had always nursed in his heart the hope of being a Trappist monk and this was his way of trying out whether this was what God wanted of him. When he arrived in Arlington in 1973, this was one of the first things he did. He made a retreat in Berryville.

Before classes started in September that year, I offered Mario a trip to Europe as a sort of prize for getting such good grades in preparatory medicine. His itinerary included Rome, the Eternal City, and Austria, Germany and France.

On his way to Vienna, somebody stole his passport, and the whole pleasure excursion became a nightmare. Because of the red tape involved in getting a new passport, Mario had to stay in Rome for many days. I have friends in Rome, among them a cardiologist, Dr. Vincenzo Ruth, and his family. They took Mario into their home and treated him like their own son. This became the most pleasant part of the whole trip. Mario ate Italian food, drank wine, and lived like a true Italian and it was a happy time for him. He had a feeling though that he would get run over by a car before he went back home to the US. And that was exactly what happened. The day before his flight for Washington, D.C., as he tried to cross the street, a car hit him. Fortunately, he was not hurt much except for a few bruises here and there.

Looking back at the whole European trip, which was meant to give him pleasure, the whole episode seemed so sad and unfortunate. But you know what Mario said when he got home? It was the best thing that happened to him in his whole life. Why? It seemed that the moment he had set foot on American soil, he had felt very inferior because he came from a poor, developing country like the Philippines, and therefore he could never adjust and be accepted as an equal by the Americans. And then he lived in Italy, where people are relatively poor when compared to Americans, but they were happy and they were on their own and they did not have to be accepted by anyone. And Mario was liberated from his feelings of inferiority and inadequacy. That was the purpose of the whole trip, as it turned out.

In Mario's journal, which he kept from 1972 to 1990, he wrote: "Love is repaid by love." In reading his journal we can chart Mario's spiritual and emotional journey in search of peace, serenity and grace. His path was often filled with questions and doubt, but even in his darkest moments, he was always able to see the light of God's goodness.

On the evening of December 31, 1972, as he pondered some personal disappointments, he wrote:

> *How often we have to remind ourselves over and over again of God's goodness if we are to keep our faith in life, in its intrinsic beauty and purposefulness. There is nothing more shattering than to see what is most precious to you ground up before the wheel of fate. There are no questions at this time, only a silent yes-the kind of yes that feels like a no, but it is the best that one can produce. All I can say is my own yes in what seems to be the senselessness of my own weakness. All I can say is yes in whatever God may want to get a yes from me, whatever kind of yes that God may require.*

While studying at Catholic University, Mario worked for a big law firm in Washington. And his whole life changed. He was exposed to corporate life, sophisticated intellectuals, high society, elegant lifestyles, clothing, travel, and so on but he continued to go to daily Mass.

His love for the Blessed Mother continued to grow. By this time, he was no longer a poor, struggling student; he was able to financially afford to order a life-size statue of the Mater Dolorosa, to be installed in my sister's chapel in our hometown. It was a beautiful statue, but Mario was not satisfied with the way her face looked and the way the tears fell from her eyes. So Mario did the face himself and worked on it until one could see the pain and the anguish and the sorrow of the Mother of God and feel these emotions in one's own heart. A single drop of tear hovered in the lower eyelid of the left eye.

Mario ordered royal robes of black velvet and white satin for the image of the Blessed Mother, but the special ones he did himself, embroidering them with gold thread, lovingly and painstakingly. He ordered a carriage covered with silver plate on the sides so that on Holy Thursday and on Easter Sunday, the image rode on it. He chose the most beautiful white silk flowers to decorate this carriage and every year for Holy Week, Mario literally showered Our Lady with great affection and tenderness. Much later, I would describe this love that Mario had for the Blessed Mother as "so deep and so real that you can almost touch it."

I grew up in the years when Catholics were praying to the Sacred Heart of Jesus, so all my life I never really felt very close to Mary and I felt guilty about it. Since Mario was my spiritual director, I asked him one day to help me love Our Lady more. He thought about this for a while and then he said: "You are a mother yourself. When someone loves your son, that makes you happy, because it is almost like loving you. So do not worry about it. Just continue loving her son, Jesus, and it is like loving her also."

I moved to Michigan in 1984 to help set up Hospice of Southeastern Michigan, but Mario continued to live in Washington. He had finished his master's degree in counseling and he had a good job with the Washington Subway Transit as a psychologist counselor to help Metro employees in their job-related problems.

In 1989, he called me up one day to say that he had a lesion on the outer part of his right thigh. I told him to see my surgeon, which he did. A biopsy was made and the diagnosis was a malignancy. I flew to Washington right away, took the slides of the frozen section and brought them to Georgetown University Hospital for a second opinion. The verdict was no malignancy, but the lymphocyte count was low and it had to be watched. We all heaved a sigh of relief and thanked God.

The following years began a battle with the lymphocyte count. Mario expressed the anguish of those years in the letters he wrote to my sister, Lucila, his favorite aunt. He called her "my second mother by affection, but my constant friend and companion in my journey to the Risen Lord."

Washington, D.C.

January 23, 1989

This is the night of my liberation. All of a sudden the veil of darkness that made my faith so painful has been lifted. I don't know where all this will lead. I only feel certain that come what may, the Lord's will be done and that is all I need to know or want to do. He does the work after all. It is just our yes that He needs. And all these years of saying yes to Him are suddenly making sense.

June 7, 1990

For a while, right after the surgery, I went through a period of severe anguish. I was terrified of any additional suffering our Lord was going to send me. And no amount of praying or talking could relieve my anxiety or depression. But on Pentecost Sunday I woke up with a glad heart which culminated in a fit of tears in church.

As we were singing the Veni Creator Spiritus, I received my courage back and a wonderful sense of expectation of the imminent arrival of the Lord. It dawned on me that I have now been placed in a position of simply waiting for God.

It was then I realized what was happening. God had restored my sense of happiness over my approaching end. I realized with a curious clarity that penetrated my soul that I was having simply to wait for God to take me home. I am discovering even more deeply that God works in simple ways that affect us profoundly. Generally speaking, the fruits of grace are instantaneous although the preparation leading up to the moment of light could take years. I really believe that on a day when I least expect it, from the gloom of the illness that I am enduring, will emerge the eternal light that I have been searching for all my life.

So now I am at peace. I no longer await death impatiently. I simply accept the fact that I will be suffering a great deal in both body and spirit before the end comes. But that, I feel, is what God wants me to do: to be ever more pliant and accepting of what He deems fit to send me. For as He constantly reminds me in the depths of my heart, there is a great piece of work He has given me to do and it can be done at this time with suffering.

I really am blessed in my relatives and friends. I find that people can't do enough for me. Fortunately, I can still manage at this time. But when the day comes when I'm truly debilitated, I have no doubt I will be surrounded by truly caring people.

June 8, 1990

Bill brought me to a lawyer's office today where I signed the papers establishing a trust fund for Mommy and dividing my assets among my heirs. It was a sad moment for me and I experienced a wave of melancholy as I walked back home. It was one of those moments when it became very clear that I'm going to die soon. All those legalities have such a way of underscoring the fact. At one point while I was walking, I recall asking sadly and rhetorically, why now when life seems so full of promise? But who are we to question the ways of God? You can imagine how quickly I made an act of faith. But the smart of it is still there especially when I remember all the lost opportunities that will never be. One of the things I realized is that I was getting depressed by trying to hang on to things as they were before I got sick. I decided that whole way of thinking was unhealthy as what I needed to do was face up to things as they are and respond to those demands.

June 11, 1990

I received your May letter today. I was so very touched by your words and your prayers! No wonder my faith is still intact and burning, despite my mounting ills. Your letter came just after I had come back from Mass where I spent a dry hour telling our Lord I was willing to put up with any suffering He wished to send.

I find that I have to work on my mindset these days. As I wrote earlier, my fear is not death. What frightens me is simply suffering of mind and body and losing my faculties. And yet this is exactly what I feel the Lord is asking of me: to offer Him my life unconditionally even if it means being ill and unable to do things for myself for a very long time, if it is God's pleasure. It frightens me to pray this way. But I persist nonetheless.

When I am most frightened, I make constant acts of faith and confidence. Added to all these, are strong and profound temptations of despair. I guess our Lord wants me to know how truly weak I am even after what I thought was a lifetime of believing. But through it all, like a theme that I hear only deep in my *heart, I'm told to trust completely, come what may, for that is how the final victory will be won.*

December 26, 1990

What I have learned through my own illness is that God sends suffering to accomplish certain very important things; and the suffering will not cease until the purpose of it is finally accomplished. This is why it takes a great deal of faith to endure the inevitable periods of darkness.

Trials are an act of love on God's part. When He sees that a soul is generous and given to Him, then He does what is necessary to make that soul grow in virtue and love. And in the later stages of spiritual development, the work is entirely God's, and His most effective tools are terrible trials of body and spirit which reveal to a soul with painful clarity and horror just how weak it is and how undeserving it is of God's love and goodness. It all sounds terribly contradictory, doesn't it?

How can you love Him who sends you pain? But this is the way it works. And the strange alchemy of sanctification actually makes suffering attractive once a certain stage of growth is achieved. The more a soul is given over to God, the more is demanded of it.

One of the peculiar things that happens to souls in trial is that they develop a certain blindness to their situation. It's all part of the darkness of spirit that the saints keep talking about. How deeply I have learned the truth of this wisdom. Christmas was very poignant to me this year.

By 1992, the diagnosis of lymphoma was made. Mario's doctor of many years told him that without specific treatment for the lymphoma, his prognosis would be limited to about two months. He opted for no chemotherapy because the doctor was not too optimistic about what it could do for him.

When Mario was about ten years old, as he and his siblings got into the car to go somewhere, I would tell the driver to be careful. And Mario would say: "Mommy, don't say that. The best thing that can happen to any one is to die so he can be with God."

Here a lifetime later, Mario was finally preparing to go home to God. He was full of joy. We were sitting in his living room one day and he asked me: "Will you be sad when I die?" I said: "I know you will be with God so I should be happy. But I will miss you." He said: "When you are sad, go shopping. I left you a little money so you can go shopping and not be sad." A few weeks after his funeral, I received a check in the mail for $10,000 with the label: "For Mommy's shopping." That was not all, however. When we opened his safety deposit box, there was a five-carat diamond solitaire labeled: "For Mommy." He never told me about it.

The day before Mario died, he called his closest friends and gave them the household or personal items that he wanted to leave them. And then he went into his library and wrote his farewell letter which he asked me to have read at his funeral Mass.

Mario wrote:

> *My dear, dear friends and beloved family, Over the years as I pondered this very difficult problem, several prospects came to my mind-the most perfect and simplest being that I am really dying. Thank you all very much for being here today. Literally, my gratitude knows no bounds. But more especially, thank you for all the goodness and openness that you have shown me during my months of trial, pain, and darkness.*
>
> *But most of all, thank you for making me brave enough during this most terrible time to be able to say yes to the Father. If you look hard through the pages of my life, you will see nothing but a soul wrenching "yes" that has been the product of many "yes-es" both big and small. In a way, a communal yes can be said by all of us, but only through the light and grace of God. For this marvelous gift, I thank you all immensely.*
>
> *So as I leave for my grave, I say yes with the gentlest of thanksgiving and yes with the most glorious of alleluias. Today you have made me triumphant.*
>
> *So good-bye my friends, my family, all who have been "yes" persons to me. For one day, we all shall say "yes" in the great grace and peace of heaven.*
>
> *Much, much love always, Mario*

He also specified that he wanted 48 white cattleya orchids and no other flowers, and he would be buried in his *barong tagalog* which his sister had ordered for him. He said he wanted his painting of Our Lady of Perpetual Help with the gold crowns on the Blessed Mother and her Son to be on top of his casket. We did all of these.

All of us kept vigil. We watched and prayed while Mario was dying. And then when he took his last breath, I had a fleeting glimpse of our Blessed Mother with arms outstretched welcoming Mario who had a beautiful smile and a look of greatest joy on his face. Was it my imagination? Or was it God's gift to console me? I'll have to ask Mario when I see him.

20

Hospice in the Philippines

In 1989, the World Health Organization (WHO), through the chief of the division of cancer and palliative care, Dr. Ian Stjernsward, was represented at the International Hospice Institute symposium on the management of terminal illness. In his presentation, Dr. Stjernsward presented very startling statistics on how 75% of the people dying in the world at that time were dying in pain, in spite of the great advances made in the control of pain, and in the management of terminal illness. He appealed to the hospice experts of the West to share their expertise in the care of the dying with the rest of the world, especially in the developing nations.

In response to this appeal, the International Hospice Institute (IHI) added a third goal to its mission. The original goals had been limited to the training of physicians on the concept of hospice care so that they can consider hospice as an option when cure of disease is no longer possible. These goals were to be achieved in two ways: through an annual symposium designed for physicians on the management of terminal illness and through the Academy of Hospice Physicians (AHP) as a forum where they can exchange ideas and information, and provide peer support for one another.

The third objective of IHI became: to help bring the concept of hospice care to the developing nations of the world so that patients dying anywhere can die painlessly, peacefully and with dignity.

I retired from my job as Director of Hospice Education, Research and Development of the Henry Ford System in October 1994. As a full time employee I could be away from my desk for only a maximum of one month, but I wanted to go to the Philippines and stay for at least four months so I could get the feel for what needed to be done in order to introduce the concept of hospice care into the country. In December 1994, I left for the Philippines not quite knowing what to do or what to expect.

According to the WHO, every country needs to understand the hospice concept so that the number of people dying in pain can be reduced to a minimum. The Philippines is a developing country so I felt that starting with the Philippines, which is my native country, the International Hospice Institute could have some basic information which can be applied to similar countries. I had the advantage of having family with whom I could stay; I knew the culture; and my previous experience of working as assistant to the secretary of health prior to my departure for the United States in 1969 would be of great help.

As a fortunate coincidence, a few years earlier, a young doctor from Manila had gone to the United States (she is married to an American) and she heard about the hospice concept. Her name is Katherine Krings. She got interested and she asked people how and where she could learn more about hospice. They told her to look for a Filipino doctor who was involved in the development of hospice programs in the United States. That was I.

Kathy looked for me and, by coincidence the IHI was having a symposium at that time. She attended the symposium and that was her real introduction to the world of hospice care. She met many of the hospice physicians who were attending the meeting as participants or faculty. She and I also became good friends, developing a mother-daughter relationship, which proved very helpful for both of us.

Kathy was working at the University of the Philippines and the Philippine General Hospital in the department of family practice, which is a very good setting for hospice care. She was also assisting the Philippine Cancer Society in its efforts to provide home care for cancer patients who were terminally ill, so already there was the nucleus of a future hospice program for these patients.

When I arrived in Manila in December 1994, all I needed to do was contact Kathy Krings, and things started to happen. Through the Philippine Cancer Society, and with the help of Dr. Krings, I was invited to give talks on the concept of hospice care to many hospitals, medical schools, medical societies, nursing schools, civic organizations, community gatherings, parish meetings, Rotary Club lunches and so on. These talks were a great opportunity to bring the idea of hospice to the many groups that had the capability to use the information for the benefit of the dying.

One important contact was established during this time. Through one of the doctors at the Philippine General Hospital, I was introduced to the undersecretary of health, Dr. Jaime Galvez-Tan. Doctor Tan is a dynamic, brilliant physician-administrator who listens to an idea, sees its potential and immediately goes to work on it. He liked the idea of hospice care for patients who were no longer curable. Through his intervention, the Secretary of Health, Dr. Juan Flavier made the statement: "Demonstrate the effectiveness and applicability of hospice care in the Philippine setting and culture in Metropolitan Manila, and I will see to it that every municipality and province of the Philippines will have hospice care."

Another important commitment was made by the Department of Health in this connection. The secretary authorized holding a national conference on hospice care in 1995 which all the medical directors of the regions of the Department of Health from all over the country, including their senior nurses and administrators, would attend. The three-day conference was a big step in the right direction for hospice care.

With the help of Dr. Krings and other physicians in Manila, we developed the conference program for early 1995. I had speakers from the United States (Dr. Stratton Hill from M.D. Anderson in Houston, Texas) and Australia (Dr. Roger Woodruff, author, oncologist and palliative care expert from Melbourne), and from Hongkong (Dr. Cynthia Goh and her staff), and of course many outstanding physicians from the Philippines. The conference was a tremendous success.

I knew how successful the national conference on hospice care was because one week after it was finished, I received an invitation from the director of the Baguio Provincial Hospital to help them launch the hospice program at the provincial hospital. It was a whole day event, with two physicians from the community assuming leadership of the project. At the evening program, the Rotary Club of Baguio pledged not only its financial and moral support for the hospice program, but said that it would develop its own core of volunteers to help take care of the hospice patients.

The saying, "From little acorns, giant oaks grow", was never more so clearly demonstrated as in the case of that one national conference on hospice care authorized by the secretary of health of the Philippines. Several years later, I would meet with groups of people who had the passion to form a hospice program in their cities or towns. Someone from their community had attended the conference, the seed had been planted, and it began to take root and was ready to bear fruit.

One such group was the little community of the University of the Philippines/ Los Banes at the foot of the Makiling Mountain in Laguna, a province 45 minutes by car from Metro Manila. Another group came from the sophisticated business district of Metropolitan Manila, in one of the most prestigious medical centers of the country, the Makati Medical Center.

Yet another group came from the province of Pampanga, in a busy little town called Guagua. This one developed later, but it was at the right time and in the right place, the Guagua National College.

Over the short period of three years, three models of how the hospice concept of care can be introduced into a developing country like the Philippines had evolved. These are the following programs: the Madre de Amor Foundation Hospice program, known also as the UP Los Banos Hospice; the hospice program in the midst of a busy cosmopolitan business district which is the model of a hospital-based hospice program: the Makati Medical Center hospice program; and the hospice program in a small town of a rice producing province called Pampanga which is the model of a college-based hospice program, the Guagua National College hospice program.

Part of my 1994-1995 experience of being in the Philippines to try to introduce the concept of hospice care into the country was an invitation to go to the campus of the University of the Philippines in Los Banos to give a talk to the community on the concept of hospice care.

God uses all types of instruments to accomplish His divine plan, and in Los Banos, it was a lady with metastatic breast cancer who had been given only a few months to live by her doctors. Her name is Tess Gonzales. She had come from Tuguegarao, Cagayan, before her husband and their grown children moved south so he could take a job at the University of the Philippines in Los Banos. Because my husband and I had lived in Tuguegarao, Cagayan, until he died in 1955, Tess knew me and this was probably the reason why I was invited to speak in Los Banos.

There had been other elements, all of which in retrospect, created a picture of amazing clarity. When I was living in Michigan, one day I had a long distance call from Hawaii. A friend of my sister, Tessie, called to get a medical opinion on her 12-year-old niece, Sarah. The little girl had recently been diagnosed with nasopharyngeal cancer, which is rare in children. Because of my training in medical oncology, it was hoped that I would have new information for the family and for Sarah.

Sarah's parents are highly educated people, both of them with Ph.D.'s from Oxford University, and both of them held important jobs at the University of the Philippines in Los Banos. Sarah's father, Fermin, was also a columnist in one of the Philippines most influential newspapers. He was also a self-proclaimed agnostic and an activist during his student days.

Sarah was everything that a gifted child could be. She was very intelligent, beautiful, and charming. She played the piano, she wrote poetry, she was the leader in her class. She was compassionate. She was the apple of her father's eye. Sarah fought against her cancer in the most agonizing way, and she died a painful death.

Day and night her parents had stayed with her both in the hospital and at home until the next hospitalization became necessary and inevitable. It could easily have been a horror story seen only in fiction movies, but it was all real: the pain, the grief, the suffering, the questions which had no answers. Except that in the midst of it all, God's grace was beginning to seep through. When Sarah finally died, Fermin found God. The agnostic became a most fervent believer.

In the midst of this terrible suffering and the indescribable sorrow that followed Sarah's death, Fermin and Dada, Sarah's mother, heard of a talk that I was going to give in St. James parish in Ayala Alabang, the parish to which my son and his family belonged. The talk was on the hospice concept of care. I did not know it at the time, but both Fermin and Dada were in the audience, sitting in front.

No one really knows what happens during occasions like that talk on hospice at St. James parish. But something happened to Fermin and Dada who suddenly found one reason for Sarah's death. They realized that God was calling them to get involved in the hospice program in Los Banos, which was then in the process of being formed. Their involvement would be their lasting memorial to Sarah. Fermin and Dada went back to Los Banos filled with zeal and determination to do all they could to help get the hospice program off the ground.

In the meantime, things were happening in other quarters. Marcia Sandoval and her husband own a beautiful summer home in Los Banos to which they invite friends during weekends to relax in the gardens and dip in the swimming pool. Marcia has two girl friends, Carol Guerrero and Ning Basa of the Pancake House chain. Carol, Ning and Marcia had felt the need to do something to help the less fortunate, but they were not sure how or when to do this. They heard about the hospice program that was in the process of being developed in Los Banos, and they were intrigued by the idea.

Their other friends, a couple from the city, Antonio Mercado and his wife, Monina, also have a farm in Laguna adjacent to the Sandovals. One nice afternoon, Marcia, Carol, and Ning were talking about hospice with Fermin and Dada Adriano. Tony Mercado was also in the group. They explained the hospice concept to him and the hospice program that was being formed in Los Banos and how they were going to be really involved in it. Tony joined the discussion and, at one point, excused himself for a few minutes. When he rejoined the group, he was informed that he had been elected president of the UP/Los Banos hospice program. He was shocked but he accepted the job. He is chairman and founder of two major advertising agencies in Manila and organization work is his mettle.

Previous to that weekend, Tony and his wife Monina were looking at the wonderful things that God had blessed them with, and they were both saying they should do something to share their blessings with others. Shortly before, Monina was in Washington, D.C., and she attended an Opus Dei meeting where the topic of hospice care was brought up. One of the ladies present, Helena Metzger, told her that the lady who was most involved in the development of hospices in the United States was a Filipina, and Monina should contact her. Monina called me when she got to Detroit and I told her that I was going to Manila in a few months.

Later Monina attended the national conference on hospice care, sponsored by the Department of Health, and she finally met me. And it was one more building block in the development of the Los Banos hospice program. Monina also met Fermin and Dada, and the impression she got was of a wonderful couple with a great zeal for hospice care, while at the same time so deeply immersed in their grief. She met them only a few weeks after the death of their daughter, Sarah.

Meanwhile Tess, the lady with metastatic breast cancer, was busy recruiting volunteers for the Los Banos hospice program. She had a big core of friends, all of them coming from the same parish, and a parish priest who was a holy man with a great sense of apostolate and ministry to the dying. Tess' group met with Fermin and Dada, and then with the group of ladies and Tony Mercado and the groundwork for a community-based hospice program in Los Banos was completed. I went to Los Banos, and in the parish hall, I conducted a training course of three sessions for the volunteers. My daughter, Nanette Magno, who had training on hospice care in the U.S., continued the training when I had to go back to the US.

The questions that were foremost in people's minds were: Where and how will terminally ill patients be referred to the Los Banos hospice program? How much will hospice care cost and how do patients pay for it? In addition to the volunteers, who will provide medical and nursing care? Will hospice have an office and who will staff it?

The answers came very simply. To invite referrals, flyers were prepared and posted in the parish church. The posters said: If you have a terminally ill patient in your family and you need care, please call this number. A telephone number of the office of the volunteer medical director was posted. Immediately, there were two referrals on the same day.

To provide medical and nursing care, the hospice program recruited a volunteer medical director to work part time with the hospice program, and a nurse to do the same.

How much will hospice care cost and how can patients pay for it? The care is provided by volunteers, so that is offered free. For medicines and supplies, the members of the board of directors of the hospice program, starting with the president, wrote checks to cover these expenses. Fund-raising events supplemented these subsidies, but personal contributions were the main source of funds.

Where will the hospice office be and who will staff it? The volunteer medical director, Dr. Rhodora del Rosario, had her office in a small place in the shopping plaza. She offered to share this with the hospice program until it had its own place.

Two years after the Los Banos hospice program was formed, Tony Mercado, the president, looked at the situation and decided the hospice program needed its own home and it would be called the Los Banos Hospice Center. He saw and managed to get a house which looked exactly the way the hospice center should look like. God had given Los Banos hospice a home of its own, with ample room for offices, community gatherings and conferences, therapy facilities and even a comfortable room for Dr. Josefina Magno when she visits. What a luxury.

Meanwhile, Fermin, the father of Sarah, succeeded in writing a book which he called: *"Oh God, Why Sarah? A father's journey into the depths of pain and faith."* The book was a success, and proceeds from its sale went to the Los Banos hospice program. Tony Mercado sent copies of the book to his corporate friends and they sent in funds by the thousands to benefit the Los Banos hospice program. A foundation, the Madre de Amor Foundation, had been created so that donors can claim tax deductions for their donations if they so desire. The Madre de Amor Foundation runs the Los Banos hospice program. At the latest count, the hospice program had taken care of 120 patients, 80 of whom had died.

Tess Gonzales, the first volunteer who started the whole thing in spite of her metastatic disease, is well and strong. Her cancer has obviously gone into remission.

A city in Metropolitan Manila, Makati is the place of big business. Banks, luxury hotels, world-class boutiques and shopping malls, wonderful restaurants, condominiums and apartment are its landmarks. In Makati also is located the Makati Medical Center, one of the most prestigious medical centers in the Philippines, staffed with the elite among the country's specialists in all fields of medicine.

My youngest son, Manny, did his internship in Makati Medical Center and at some point, he was president of the interns club of the hospital. I was invited to give a talk there on the hospice concept of care during one of my visits to the Philippines. The hall was packed with doctors, residents, interns, medical students and nurses. And, most importantly, the chairman of the Makati Medical Center, Dr. Raul Fores, was present.

Doctor Fores is a brilliant surgeon and a deeply spiritual individual. He loved the concept of hospice care and immediately, he enlisted my help in developing a hospice home care program for the hospital. He and I worked on the plans and the fastest way by which the program could get started.

Having the top man in an organization interested in an idea can make the difference between success and failure in the implementation of something like a hospital-based hospice program. Nurses, physicians, and support staff are already on the payroll of the hospital and it becomes a question of identifying those who can deal effectively with terminally ill patients. Doctor Fores was very supportive and it did not take too long before the Makati Medical Center hospice program was a reality. It was given an office on the ground floor of the hospital. A physician on the staff, Dr. Reynaldo Nambayan III, was assigned as medical director. In addition, two nurses and a social worker were designated as members of the hospice team. A secretary was appointed.

What was lacking in Makati were the volunteers who are a very important part of hospice care. It was in this area where Doctor Nambayan, the medical director, played a very important role. He personally helped in the recruiting of volunteers and he designed a training program which would prepare them to help in the care of terminally ill patients and their families, following the concepts of hospice care. I was very impressed when, at a Christmas program for hospice patients and families, which was organized by volunteers, almost one hundred people participated. Forty of them were volunteers, all of them active in caring for hospice patients in their homes.

The Makati Medical Center hospice program is strictly for indigent patients of the hospital who have been discharged home because cure is no longer possible. It is a good beginning. Two US trained neurologists who are experts in pain management have joined the hospice team. More volunteers are being trained. Dr. Nambayan and the hospice nurses have gone to Australia for more advanced training in hospice care. It is hoped that in the very near future, the Makati Medical Center Hospice Program can be expanded to serve also the needs of the paying patients of the hospital who need hospice care.

For now, the Makati Medical Center Hospice Program can serve as a model for a hospital-based hospice home care program. The ideas, which have been successfully employed in this program, can very well be replicated in other hospitals which have a similar philosophy in terms of caring for their patients until the moment of death.

Pampanga is a rice-producing province north of Manila, about an hour's drive by car when the weather is good and there are no traffic jams. On both sides of the superhighway are verdant fields of rice, dotted here and there with nipa huts where the farmers live.

In Pampanga, there is a small, very busy town called Guagua. The town is picturesque, a showcase of how communities evolved from the Spanish times. The centerpiece is the Catholic Church, made of concrete, built to last for generations. Around the church is the town plaza with the market, stores and houses of the prominent residents. Snuggled into this picture is the Guagua National College, a family-owned private school which started as a small school and over the years had blossomed into a national college with master's degree and Ph.D. programs in education and philosophy.

The president of Guagua National College is a retired brigadier general, Rafael Goseco, a highly respected gentleman in both government and private circles. His wife, Pet Goseco, is an academician, with a Ph.D. in linguistics. She was dean of the college of linguistics in the University of the Philippines. The Gosecos are my very good friends.

Pet Goseco travels to Guagua every Monday to give doctrine classes to the faculty members of the Guagua National College who have an interest in their spiritual formation. I became interested in how she conducts these classes because I felt it would be useful for everyone to know how to give them. Pet was very happy to do this for me, so she and her husband and my sister Noli planned a whole day affair with a fancy lunch in Clark Field, then an attractive place to visit and to shop in, before proceeding to Guagua.

In the course of the preparations, Pet happened to ask if I would like to give a talk on hospice care while we were in Guagua. Why not? So she informed her husband and when we arrived in the school, we found out that a word from the president of the college can immediately result in a major convocation. The hall was packed with faculty, students, community leaders and many others. This was the audience that heard about the concept of hospice care for the first time in June 1998.

What happened after that talk was almost like a miracle. A group of faculty members, most of them deans and senior administrative officials, decided that hospice care is needed, not only in Guagua, but also in the whole province. And they went to work. The school physician happened to be also a municipal health physician employed by the Department of Health, so she had access to all the physicians of that category in the province. The principal of the grade school and her husband have leadership roles among the neighborhood community organizations called *barangay* which look after the welfare of their respective groups. The rest of the core group represented Eucharistic ministers of the diocese, and other religious organizations.

I made several more visits to Guagua National College in the course of ten months. During this period of time, the Guagua National College hospice program became a legal entity. The papers had been filed with the Securities and Exchange Commission (SEC). The medical director had been meeting with other physicians in the area, the *barangay* captains had been assembled and given a briefing on what the hospice concept is, and their respective roles in its implementation; the Eucharistic ministers had enlisted the support of the archbishop of the diocese and he had promised to help. Fund-raising activities had been planned for the year. A training program for young volunteers, the high school students, is in the process of being developed.

As part of the efforts of the International Hospice Institute to develop models which may be replicated not only in the Philippines, but also in other developing countries with similar needs, the Guagua National College Hospice Program can very well be one of such models. Because the core group, which was responsible for developing the program in such a relatively short time, are all academicians, it became easy to document every step that had been taken, so that this information can be shared with others.

The Guagua National College had another convocation in March 1999. The main feature was hospice care, but an important segment of the program was an academic interchange during which the students asked many questions about the subject. Most of them were high school students and it was very gratifying to hear these young people, the future leaders of the country, talk about their insights into the topic of death and how it can be made more acceptable and less frightening, with the help of hospice volunteers and caregivers.

21

My spiritual journey

It was the second to the last day of 1998, and in the Philippines, it is called Rizal Day, in honor of our national hero, Jose Rizal. A movie of his life had been in the newspapers for many weeks and I wanted to see it. My daughter-in-law, her sister, my ten-year-old granddaughter and I all trooped to the movie house at 1:00 in the afternoon after a quick lunch in the mall. It was all exciting and great fun, something which I had not done in all the time I had lived in the United States.

The movie was more than three hours long and we had to rush to another side of the mall to get to our car. On the way out, I felt very tired, my heart was pounding, and I could hardly catch my breath. I asked that we sit down for a while to rest and we all did.

We got home and I sat on a chair in the living room, had the electric fan overhead turned on and I waited for the not-feeling-well moments to pass away. They did not. I began to sense that I was in some kind of trouble. I called my daughter who lived about ten minutes away and told her my heart did not feel normal. She came immediately, felt my pulse and then rushed me to a medical clinic inside the village where we all lived, which is open 24 hours a day for emergencies.

The doctor and the nurse on duty had me lie down, hooked me to an electrocardiograph, listened to my heart and got all excited. The doctor tried very hard to be calm and professional, and he said his recommendation was for me to go by ambulance to the nearest hospital. He placed me on oxygen and put an IV line and I asked why, and he said they may have to put me on emergency medication. Meanwhile, my daughter got busy on the telephone to contact a cardiologist, arrange for an ambulance and notify my family. Then she handed me my rosary saying: "So you will have something to keep you busy while waiting."

My son and my daughter-in-law had arrived by then and I heard my son say: "Mommy is so cool." In the jargon of the young generation, that could mean a lot of things. But I did feel "cool." I was very peaceful and I prepared myself for death and I was not afraid at all. I always worried about all my children and what would happen to them when I died; but at that moment in the village clinic, those thoughts never entered my mind. I was completely and totally in the hands of God, my loving Father.

The ambulance came and before too long, we were on our way to the nearest hospital which was the most acceptable to me and my family. Traffic in Manila has no comparison anywhere in the world. Streets can easily look like giant parking lots, with cars just sitting there not moving for hours. The ambulance ride, however, was something like a small miracle. With lights flashing and sirens blaring, we were in the hospital in 15 minutes, a ride that could easily take an hour or two on an ordinary day.

The physician on emergency duty took over very efficiently and competently, and did all the procedures necessary while waiting for the cardiologist to arrive. He also got excited because my blood pressure had shot up to very dangerous levels and it wouldn't go down in spite of the sublingual medications. Meanwhile, my electrocardiogram was going like crazy. He was asking me many questions: did I have a headache? Did I feel dizzy? Did I have chest pains? I did not know if I had a headache or if I felt dizzy, but I knew I did not have chest pains.

Then the cardiologist arrived. He examined my heart and lungs, looked at all the machines and decided I needed to be in the intensive care unit. He assured me that if my other tests were normal, he would let me go home the following day so I could spend New Year's Eve with my family. Then I was wheeled into the ICU. My children were following, but at the threshold of the unit, they were politely told to go home, but to be sure to leave a phone number so they can be contacted immediately if something happens.

This was the worst moment of the whole episode. No one knew then what could happen to me. I could die, and all I wanted was to have my children with me to hold my hand and to say goodbye. I wanted them to be with me so I could tell them things that they needed to know, but the system asked them to leave and I was all alone. It was true that I had many nurses every time I needed something or to check on the IV or the cardiac monitor, but to them I was just another patient, admitted on an emergency to the ICU. It was the loneliest night of my life.

They did more tests, and morning came. My cardiologist arrived and he was pleased with the results and then he said the most welcome words in the English language: "You may go home."

I look back on the whole episode and all I can think of are two things: God had a purpose for it and the ICU is the loneliest place in the world. Intensive care need not be so, for the sake of patients and their families. Being in the ICU was also an opportunity for me to think about my spiritual life, my relationship with God.

For some years after my husband died, I continued with my daily Mass, Rosary, prayers—all the practices that characterize a good Catholic life. In retrospect, I was the typical mechanical Catholic who did all the right things, but never had a real personal relationship with Christ. God was a stern Father who was far away, and you do not bother Him with the trivia of every day existence.

Then in the 60s, *Cursillo* in Christianity came to the Philippines. This was a three-day course conducted by a rector and a spiritual director and six or more lay people called *rollistas* because they delivered lectures called *rollos*. The movement originated in Spain, and it took the country by storm. People went to the course, for some reason or another, usually forced by well-meaning friends. They went in unbelieving and they came out totally transformed.

I was invited several times to attend a course but I always refused, saying in my heart: I am fine, I do not need anything to renew me. Oh, the arrogance and the complacency. One friend came to my office one day and she said the *Cursillo* would be good for me because I was in a position of authority; and if I meet Christ face to face, I could influence people working with me to do the same.

I did go, and the three days completely changed my life. I literally met Christ face to face, and I began to feel the joy of knowing Him personally as a friend, a brother, someone who loves me and cares about me. And I saw God as a loving Father and myself as His daughter.

The *Cursillo* became an important part of my spiritual life. I became *a rollista*, then a rector, and I served on many, many weekends. For many years, I enjoyed being part of this important means of renewal in the Catholic Church.

Then I left for the United States. I shed tears of sadness because I was going to leave this apostolate in which God in His goodness had allowed me a part.

As soon as I got settled in the US, I started to look for the *Cursillo* Center in America, so I could renew my involvement in the movement. Several months passed, and I still had no clue. Then one day, I was at a cocktail party and a gentleman approached me and asked if I was from the Philippines and if I knew a certain individual. He said he had become friends with this man through the *Cursillo* and he wanted to get in touch with him. My search had finally brought results because in no time at all, I was in touch with the *Cursillo* leaders in the US.

We were living in Arlington, Virginia, at the time; the community was across the Potomac River. We had made friends and before too long, I was involved in organizing *Cursillo* weekends in our community. Again I gave *rollos*, I was rector, and we had the monthly Mass and follow-up meetings in my home.

In one of the *Cursillo* meetings several months later, I overheard some of the girls talking about the Holy Spirit and speaking in tongues. I was fascinated and I wanted to know what these were all about. One of the girls offered to take me to a prayer meeting which were at the time just being started at the Catholic University. I did go and I did hear people speaking in tongues and others interpreting the messages. It was all new to me and I did not really know what to make out of what was happening.

After that particular meeting, some 12 of the members of the group asked me to go to the chapel so they could pray over me and so that I would receive the gift of the Holy Spirit. I tried to refuse, saying I was not prepared. They insisted, so I went along. They laid hands on me and prayed over me, some in tongues, some in vocal prayer for about ten minutes. Then I was told that if I found myself speaking in tongues, I should not hold it back because that is God's gift to me. I politely said yes, but in my heart I did not believe.

Three months later, my daughter had an emergency appendectomy at Providence Hospital in Washington. It was about eight o'clock at night and I was sitting beside her bed praying. Suddenly she said to me: "Mommy, you are praying in tongues." I went to the chapel and when I opened my mouth, I was indeed praying in tongues. I did not tell anyone. This "gift of tongues" was characteristic of the charismatic movement of the early 1970's. It is difficult to describe or explain. Some people receive it and some do not, even after many years in the movement. I can only call it one of God's mysterious ways.

We all know that when God gives us a gift, it is not because we deserve it. He has a purpose for giving that particular gift and I saw it soon enough.

We had a party in my home when, in the middle of the party, I heard some of my friends arguing loudly in the dining room. I asked what was going on and one of the guys said he was very insulted when people tell him about speaking in tongues and expecting him to believe it. I said: "It is true." These were my friends who love me and who respect me because I am a doctor and a scientist, so a great silence greeted my announcement. Then I said: "There is only one way to find out. Why don't you all go to a prayer meeting and see for yourself what is going on there?"

They went, and out of that group, three became the most active leaders of the charismatic movement in Washington. That was the reason why God had given me the gift, and not because I deserved it.

I belonged to St. Agnes parish in Arlington, Virginia. I remember that before we had looked for a house to rent or buy, I had made a visit to this church and I loved it very much so I told the Lord that if it would be possible, may we please belong to this parish? He answered my prayers.

I was coming out of St. Agnes church one Saturday morning after Mass when I heard someone behind me call my name. I turned around and I saw this lady whom I did not know. She said: "I have been wanting to know you for a long time. I wonder if we may have coffee whenever you have time?" I had nothing planned for that morning so I said we could do it then. I was embarrassed that I did not know her name since she seemed to know me quite well, so instead of asking her directly, I asked to look at her missal, which I was sure had her name somewhere. True enough, there it was: Helena Metzger. She drove us in her car to a beautiful mansion on top of a small hill and she left me in the huge living room while she prepared the coffee. There on top of the coffee table were all kinds of printed pamphlets and brochures on Opus Dei. Over coffee, I asked her if she was connected to Opus Dei and of course she was. In retrospect, the whole invitation to meet me was for the purpose of introducing me to Opus Dei. The conversation was light, and Helena did not do any hard selling. She really just wanted to be my friend, but we talked a little about what Opus Dei is: trying to be a contemplative in the world. I had told her that I was extremely busy and that I felt I was all right in terms of my spiritual life, and she understood. However, in subsequent months and weeks, she would invite me to small gatherings of around 20 people in her home to give a talk on hospice care. And then she would invite me to go to a day of recollection, which would occupy one morning. And then she would arrange for me to go to a three-day retreat with some other ladies. She would drive us to wherever the retreat was taking place, we would have a good dinner on our way, and the whole experience became one of pleasure and camaraderie. The other activities continued: the small groups with a speaker, the days of recollection, Confession, retreats and so on. Before too long, I had the option to be a cooperator, someone who supports the activities and apostolate of Opus Dei with prayers, sacrifice, and financial contribution at one's discretion, and within one's means, big or small. The important thing was to make a commitment in order to demonstrate one's support. I told Helena I would like to be a cooperator of Opus Dei for the next 50 years of my life.

What I did not know was that God had His own plans for me. In 1987, I went to Rome for the canonization of Saint Lorenzo Ruiz de Manila, the first Filipino saint. One of the activities of the canonization was a reception at Collegio Filipino. I was sitting in the waiting room of the Collegio when a distinguished-looking Italian priest sat across from me and asked me: "Are you a member of the Work?" I said: "No, Father. Sometimes I do feel that I have a vocation to Opus Dei, but I do not have the time nor the inclination to join." He smiled gently and said: "I felt exactly the way you feel several years ago. I am a chemist, and I felt the call, but I did not want to do anything about it. Now, I would not know what to do with my life without Opus Dei." He smiled again and said: "I will pray for you."

His prayers and those of many others went up to God and touched His heart, because not too long afterwards, I started to think about Opus Dei. I had been going to the center in Chicago every Saturday to take part in the activities there because we did not have a center in Michigan. Slowly my plans to continue being a cooperator for 50 years began to change. I continued making the retreats and the seminars of Opus Dei and slowly, these became part of my life.

In one of the retreats in Indiana in 1990, the directress talked with me and asked if I had considered being a member of Opus Dei. She gave me a sheet of paper and said if in my prayer I find that I would like to be a member, I could write a letter to the vicar to express my desire. Two nights later, I wrote the letter and handed it to the directress. Gone were my doubts and my anxieties and my plea of being too busy. The Holy Spirit had worked His miracle in my soul.

From the life and writings of Blessed Josemaria Escriva, the founder of Opus Dei, three things in particular keep me going in my daily life. The first is the practice of saying *Serviam*, I will serve. To me this is a strong reminder of the lesson which Jesus taught us at the Last Supper. Without saying a word, He placed a towel around His waist, poured water into a basin and began to wash the feet of His disciples. They were appalled but He said: "If I, the Lord and Master, have washed your feet, you should also wash each other's feet. I have given you an example that you may copy what I have done to you."

Jesus wants us to serve others and saying *Serviam* reminds me of this every day. To be what Jesus wants us to be, we must be servants to others. I must use whatever talents God gives me to be of service to others. This thought keeps me going as I struggle in my spiritual life.

The second idea I have learned from Blessed Josemaria is to try to be always aware that God is my Father and I am His daughter. We are all children of God and consequently we must try to live in the presence of God day and night. The thought that God is my Father assures me that He is always with me. Whatever I do, say, think or feel must always be for God. Whatever activity I am involved in, I will not be afraid because God is with me and He will help me. Nothing is impossible with God, so I can trust Him completely and be able to say with all my heart and soul: "Thy will be done, Lord."

I have also learned in Opus Dei that my work is the work of God. Whatever our work is as a doctor, janitor, housewife, student and so on, that work can be offered to God. Therefore, everything I do must be done to the best of my ability and the work that I do must be as perfect as I can make it. As a doctor, I must be the best doctor I can be. That is the way I can sanctify my work and at the same time sanctify myself and, by the grace of God, sanctify others who work with me.

These directions, which I have learned in Opus Dei, allow me to keep a personal relationship with Jesus. In addition, mental prayer-30 minutes in the morning and 30 minutes in the afternoon-gives me the chance to have daily one-on-one conversations with Jesus. I tell Him everything that bothers me, all the anxieties I have about my children and their needs, the frustrations in my work, all my concerns.

Our daily norms of piety, the study circle each week, the monthly recollection, the yearly seminar and retreat—all these bring me new reminders of God's love and enable me to grow in my love for Him. Also the friendship and the affection that my sisters show me in Opus Dei make the love of Jesus a living reality which strengthens my personal relationship with Him.

In what way does hospice work fit into the spirituality of Opus Dei? Blessed Josemaria emphasized the importance of each and every soul, for whom Jesus died. As children of God and friends of Jesus, we must always be looking for souls to bring to God. Hospice work, which is sometimes termed as being a midwife for souls, consists precisely in bringing souls to God in those crucial last moments before they meet Him face to face. Hospices thus help souls to be born into eternal life.

Hospice work is the particular work that God has given to me and it is in doing hospice work that I should achieve holiness. Apostolate with the dying is tremendous work.

While busy with day-to-day work required to meet the needs of the body, many people neglect or relegate to low priority the needs of the soul. As life perceptively comes to an end during serious illness, these people have the chance to finally look at the needs of the soul and to reach out to God.

Hospice workers are in a position to provide the spiritual help and guidance, which the dying person needs. We can pray together, express love, sorrow and thanks to God and, to Catholics, bring the last sacraments of Penance, Holy Anointing and the Eucharist.

God really was a hound of heaven to me when He called me to Opus Dei, because I tried not to listen for a long time. When I finally did, at seemingly such a late hour, I realized that I was one of the laborers in the vineyard parable, just standing around and doing nothing until close to the end of the working day. They worked and got the same pay as those who have been working since the first hour. I am grateful for this.

In Opus Dei, I learned a Latin expression which has become my favorite: *Nunc coepi,* "now I begin". I often feel that I am not getting anywhere, but in Opus Dei, I have learned that every day, every moment, right now, I begin again.

Postscript: Josefina B Magno died July 27th 2003 in Manila in the hospital, She had been admitted for congestive heart failure and was with family when she died. She telephoned as many overseas family members as she could reach to tell us that she loved us and was at peace, and would pray for us.

Jo Magno did not want this journal published until after her death. She was 84 and still had many ideas and plans and was more interested in "doing" than finishing her book. However, she did complete it, as an act of faith.

Jo Magno leaves a legacy of caring that sustains more than just those whose lives she touched as a hospice physician. Her inspiration was legendary and her faith that of a living saint. It is for this reason that we, her children, decided to publish these memoirs of her life, her hospice work, and her devotion to God. I can hear her say it now....

"God is so Good!"

Margaret Day Magno, for the family
June 26, 2007

978-0-595-45651-2
0-595-45651-0

Printed in the United States
91973LV00004B/346-360/A